DANISH YEARBOOK
OF
PHILOSOPHY

VOLUME 26

DANISH YEARBOOK OF PHILOSOPHY

VOLUME 26

1991

MUSEUM TUSCULANUM PRESS
UNIVERSITY OF COPENHAGEN 1991

published for
The Society for Philosophy and Psychology, Copenhagen,
in cooperation with
the Philosophical Societies of Aarhus and Odense
and with financial support from
the Danish Research Council for the Humanities

*

EDITORIAL BOARD:

DAVID FAVRHOLDT	FINN COLLIN	UFFE JUUL JENSEN
University of Odense	University of Copenhagen	University of Aarhus
Chairman		
ARNE GRØN	KLEMENS KAPPEL	SVEN ERIK NORDENBO
University of Copenhagen	Secretary	University of Copenhagen
	C. H. KOCH	
	University of Copenhagen	

*

Articles for consideration and all editorial communications should be sent in five copies to:
Danish Yearbook of Philosophy
University of Copenhagen, Department of Philosophy
Njalsgade 80, DK 2300 Copenhagen S, Denmark

Business communications, including subscriptions and orders for reprints, should
be addressed to the publishers:
MUSEUM TUSCULANUM PRESS
Njalsgade 94
DK 2300 Copenhagen S
Denmark

*

© 1991 DANISH YEARBOOK OF PHILOSOPHY
COPENHAGEN, DENMARK
PRINTED IN DENMARK
BY SPECIAL-TRYKKERIET VIBORG A-S

ISBN 87-7289-124-6
ISSN 0070-2749

CONTENTS

Finn Collin: *Translation and Foreign Cultures* 7
W. Robert Pulvertaft: *Population Ethics. On Parfit's Views Concerning Future Generations* 33
Mogens Blegvad: *"Value" in Turn-of-the-Century Philosophy and Sociology* 51
C. H. Koch: *The Correspondence of Ernst Mach with a Young Danish Philosopher* 97

TRANSLATION AND FOREIGN CULTURES

FINN COLLIN

University of Copenhagen

I

In this article I discuss the view that interpretation of the language of a radically foreign culture is impossible, and that the thought of such a culture must hence remain unfathomable to us; a philosophical doctrine with obvious and embarrassing implications for anthropology and history. For these disciplines are *inter alia* concerned with providing us with accounts of the modes of thinking of alien peoples, whether in distant times or in remote regions of the world. And without a proper grasp of these peoples' thoughts, in a narrow sense, we have no adequate grasp either of their intentions, desires or actions: We are reduced to recording only the most extrinsic, behavioural aspects of their culture. For convenience, I shall refer to the view that such transcultural understanding is impossible as the *Hermetic Thesis*, the thesis that foreign cultures are hermetically closed to each other.[1]

At the outset we must clear up an ambiguity in the Hermetic Thesis as it has been propounded in the literature. Sometimes a strong claim is advanced, to the effect that the *learning* of a language creates insurmountable obstacles to a member of a radically alien culture; at other times only the weaker claim is made that exact *translation* cannot be attained. The latter position is compatible with the admission that the language which defies translation can still be *learnt* by the alien. In this article, I shall examine the weaker position only. This is in part because I consider this to be the most plausible version, although I would oppose the view, which some might hold, that the stronger position may be rejected out of hand as flying in the face of established fact. One would be the fact that anthropologists have been known to go into the jungle and crack the code of tribal societies whose cultural stage represents the starkest possible contrast with the anthropologists. But this alleged fact might be disputed on the grounds that the anthropologists have only managed to conform to native discourse in its purely external, behavioural aspect, while failing to penetrate the meaning which it embodies. Such a sceptical conception can be given precise meaning on the basis of a realist semantics, in the Dummettian sense, countenancing verification-transcendent meanings. But this leads to the primary reason why I bypass the stronger version of the Hermetic Thesis here: The reasoning in favour of this view would closely parallel the one I shall offer below as the strongest argument for the translational variant of that thesis. Hence, to avoid tedious repetition, I shall confine myself to one deployment of this reasoning. Its application to the stronger position will be obvious from the use to which I put it below; so will the way in which it can be countered.

II

To examine the weak version of the Hermetic Thesis, we must first agree on what is to be understood by a translation. In the debate over translatability, authors have often arrived at contradictory conclusions on the basis of identical arguments and examples, due to the fact that they impose different constraints upon the notion of translation.[2] And often such constraints have not been explicitly spelled out. A clarification is needed. Trivially and minimally, a translation is a pairing of meaning-equivalent expressions from different languages. We may raise this a little beyond triviality by plugging in a substantive theory of meaning, namely the theory which construes meaning as a function of truth or satisfaction conditions (with or without an additional requirement that these conditions be epistemically accessible); translation is then made out to be the pairing of expressions, from different languages, with identical truth or satisfaction conditions.

But presumably the ordinary notion of translation goes further than this. We would hardly call a large and intricately interwoven set of sentences of one language a translation of an atomic sentence of another language (i.e. a sentence not subject to further analysis in that language), despite coincidence of truth conditions, nor would we accept a highly complex term of the first language as a translation of a simple term in the second. An example might be the terms "seven" and "$27-45+5^2$" which have identical satisfaction conditions in all possible worlds but which do not intuitively translate each other. Some additional requirement of identical logical form seems to be at play, a notion related to Carnap's concept of intensional isomorphism, calling for the aligned expressions to have identical decompositions into atomic semantic parts. Perhaps it could even be maintained that our everyday notion of translation calls for *grammatical* equivalence, too: a passive construction in the translated language must not be mapped into an active construction in the translating language, even if the two have identical truth conditions. Moreover, specialized concerns call for even stronger, specialized versions of translation. In translating poetry, we may want to preserve the metre of the original, and to match the emotional values of its terms.

These deliberations remind us that what we require from a translation varies systematically with different uses; and our task here is thus to pick a version which is germane to the anthropologist's and historian's concerns. Such a notion will belong in the liberal end of the spectrum; indeed, it will be so liberal as perhaps to make the term "translation" somewhat misleading. Yet this is a purely verbal point. The substantive issue is whether the notion of meaning specification which we adopt is relevant to the anthropologist's and historian's business. We might characterize this as the business of conveying the content of the thought and action of alien peoples and historical characters by purely verbal, discursive means; as opposed to, say, getting someone to understand other peoples by placing him among them and have him learn the facts on his own accord. Anthropology and history are organized bodies of assertions about the world, not techniques for achieving understanding; hence their results must be expressible in discursive form.

We are about to examine certain semantic facts which are thought to represent a threat to anthropology and history, thus construed; hence the notion of "translation" with which we operate should be such that the failure to achieve translation, in this sense, would indeed constitute an embarrassment to these disciplines. Translation as the pairing of intensionally isomorphic expressions is not such a notion, nor is the notion of translation as the faithful replication of emotive meaning and metre. To the extent that the anthropologist or the historian are concerned to provide us with a grasp of the thoughts contained in a certain stretch of the aliens' discourse, what they are called upon to do is to produce some text in their own language which possesses the same truth conditions as the selected stretch of discourse, and the same inferential interconnections with other such stretches; structural, grammatical and metrical correspondence being of no moment.

Indeed they need deliver even less than this: What they have to do, minimally, is to tell us some story about the elements of which that discourse is composed which will reveal the semantically relevant aspects of their use, i.e. the truth conditions and the inferential interconnections between sentences. Such an account need not consist of sentences which are synonymous with those native sentences the truth conditions of which they indicate: It will not primarily *cite* equivalent sentences in the two languages, but will *use* the home language to specify the semantically relevant facts about the way native sentences are used; in the processs employing semantic vocabulary which is not a part of the native sentences examined. The home language is used primarily as a metalanguage for the description of the native language, not as another object language with which that language is aligned. Note that this technique is not all that different from the way in which standard dictionaries of synonyms spell out the fine shades of meaning of related terms: They will provide an account of the general meaning which either term conveys and go on to state the specific implications of selecting one term rather than another, making free use of semantic meta-vocabulary. The overall account is hardly *synonymous* with the term examined.

In brief, on the broader reading of "translation", our question will be whether the meaning of alien sentences and terms can be conveyed verbally in the anthropologist's or historian's language. That such a rendition of meaning may not be what we ordinarily call a "translation" is a purely terminological worry. The only legitimate complaint about the suggested notion, once it is granted that it is relevant to the anthropologist's or the historian's business, would be the charge that it is so liberal as to make "translation" trivially attainable between any two natural languages. But we shall se that this worry is unfounded as far as the present suggestion is concerned.

III

First, I must take issue with an influential argument which, if true, would allow us to bring our investigation to a close before it really got started. This argument tries to show, on the basis of very abstract *a priori* idea, that a guarantee can be given that even the remotest language must necessarily allow of translation into the historian's or anthropologist's idioms. The argument is set forth by Donald Davidson in the article, "On the Very Idea of a Conceptual Scheme".[3] Or perhaps one should talk of "arguments" rather than "argument"; for there is a certain doubt as to the precise thrust of Davidson's reasoning, which seems to oscillate between the charge that we cannot give intelligible content to the idea of a language untranslatable into ours, and the different objection that we could have no evidence for the existence of such a language; more precisely, the objection that any evidence ostensibly showing that some language was untranslatable into the home idiom would *eo ipso* count as evidence that this was not a language after all. I believe that Davidson's argument fails on either reading, but shall devote attention only to the former.

Davidson's first line of argument may be set forth as follows, with considerable simplification: Possession of a truth value is the constitutive feature of the notion of (assertoric) language. We can only give precise and non-metaphorical sense to the idea of an assertoric language by representing it as a structure the constituents of which – i.e., sentences – may be true, or false. Now the only general handle we have upon the notion of truth is Tarski's Convention T, which says that any satisfactory theory of truth for some language L must enable us to infer, for any sentence s of L, a theorem of the form "s is true if and only if p", where "s" is replaced by a structural description of s and "p" by s itself, if L is English, and by a translation of s into English, if it is not. In other words, Convention T establishes an essential tie between the notion of truth for a foreign language L and the idea of translation of L into the home language. We cannot break this connection without setting the notion of truth entirely adrift. And the notion of truth, we agreed, is constitutive of the notion of assertoric language. So it seems that we must insist on the translatability, in principle, of anything deserving to be called a language.

This argument smacks of sophistry, and so we may be forgiven for countering it with a manoeuvre with an artificiality of its own. My artifice is that of constructing a new language which fuses the object language L and English; dub this language Lenglish. All well-formed sentences of English are sentences of Lenglish, as are all well-formed sentences of L. Besides, sentences of L may be joined with sentences of English by the "if and only if"-connective to form biconditionals of Lenglish. Finally, quotation marks may be put around sentences of Lenglish, with the same effect as in English. The point of these stipulations, of course, is to permit, as well-formed sentences of Lenglish, sentences of the form "s is true if and only if p", where the embedded expressions are replaced by expressions from L. Given the legitimacy of such hybrids, we can offer the following schematic procedure for the construction of a truth definition for L, couched in Lenglish as a metalanguage, which trivially satisfies Convention T: For any sentence s of L, frame an axiom of the form, "s is true if and only if p", where s is to be replaced by a structural description of s and p is replaced by s itself.

The thing to appreciate is that this recipe is intelligible even to a person who is incapable of translating sentences of L into English. It provides him with a grasp of the notion of true-in-L, i.e. a grasp of the way in which a theory of truth for L, designed according to this recipe, will satisfy the Tarskian condition, compliance with which is precisely that which makes it a theory of *truth*. The ability to translate the sentences which are plugged into the biconditionals is not required for, and would add nothing to, the understanding of the notion of true-in-L which emerges from the outlined procedure. Admittedly, being ignorant of the meaning of s, such a person would not learn from the biconditionals wherein the truth conditions of any particular sentences of L consists. But then the recipe is not meant to provide him with the actual truth conditions of any specified sentence (although any axiom of a truth theory constructed according to the recipe will, of course, specify such conditions), but only with a general grasp of the notion of true-in-L. In the same spirit, we need not worry about the complaint that, so long as we do not possess a recursive characterization of sentencehood in L, we shall not be capable of actually designing a truth theory for L, since we cannot specify in a general way the class of items which are to be plugged into the Tarskian formula. For, once again, the above recipe does give us a grasp of what it means, given any assertoric sentence x, for x to be true if x belongs to L. This illumination flows from the abstract specification of how the truth theory is to be constructed, and from the insight that, and how, this theory will satisfy the Tarskian condition. The actual implementation of the recipe would add nothing to this understanding.

At this point the second line of argument in Davidson's article might be brought into play: The point, he might insist, is not really that we cannot say in the abstract what truth would consist in for an untranslatable language, but that we could never *establish* that somebody spoke a language untranslatable into ours. In order to establish that a certain segment of the aliens' behaviour counts as a language, we would have to establish that the concept of truth applies to it; and this presupposes the construction of a translation of the supposed language into our own idiom, thus defeating the untranslatability claim. In other words, we could never establish that some segment of alien behaviour amounted to the speaking of a language untranslatable into our own tongue, since the evidence would either confirm that we were indeed dealing with a language, but then a translatable one, or would confirm the suspicion of intranslatability, but at the price of undermining the assumption that the behaviour in question counted as language use at all. Thus, the idea of a language untranslatable into our own is one which must always have the evidence against it, in the nature of the case.

Against this argument, two points may be made. In the first place, Davidson's reasoning overlooks the distinction that was drawn in an earlier section, viz. that between being able to translate a language and being able to *learn* it. After having spent some time with the aliens, we might gradually find ourselves capable of responding appropriately to their utterances, and even of responding in the same tongue, while still finding the things said resistant to translation into our old idiom. This experience would provide ample evidence that the aliens do indeed have a language, but an untranslatable one. It would be no use for Davidson to object that (radical) interpretation presupposes large-scale agreement in beliefs between interpreter and interpretee, this in turn presupposing semantic identity between the sentences, from either language, which express those beliefs. For the beliefs which the interpreter attributes to the natives need not be beliefs he held in advance, and could express in his old language, but might be beliefs which he forms in the process of getting enculterated in the alien society, participating in native activities, etc. This, after all, is the way that first languages are learnt; and presumably second languages can be learnt in the same way, too.

Secondly, the argument seems to presuppose a verificationist (anti-realist) premise, to the effect that we cannot make sense of facts, *in casu* facts concerning the semantics of an alien language, which are cognitively inaccessible to us. Yet such a premise is contentious, and calls for a defense. Alternatively, Davidson might try to get by on a weaker premise, to the effect that *semantic* facts must always be so accessible. Such a claim has sometimes been advanced, under the title of the "publicity principle". But even this premise calls for an argument.

Thus Davidson's quick way of disposing of the translatability question cannot be sustained. However, as we shall se below, it is true that once an anti-realist premise is adopted, the conclusion that translation must be possible is indeed favoured. However, the case needs a much more elaborate argument than Davidson supplies.

IV

The most powerful and interesting arguments used to show that cross-cultural translation is impossible revolve around the idea of *the pervasive theory-ladenness of language*. This is the idea that the meanings of linguistic terms are in part a function of the theories (beliefs, assumptions) they serve to express. There is no neutral "data vocabulary" common to all languages, it is said, and *a fortiori* no shared basic vocabulary in terms of which the higher and ostensibly divergent strata of different languages can be reduced to a common semantic denominator. The belief in sentences the assessment of which as true or false involves no cognitive processing or inference is a pernicious myth engendered by bad epistemology. This is not to deny that there is such a thing as ascertaining how things are by means of the senses, nor that the outcome of this process can be expressed in something appropriately called "observation sentences", which are distinctive in evoking uniform acceptance or rejection from speakers upon confrontation with identical sensory evidence. Observation sentences enjoy this epistemic privilege not because they lack an inferential component and hence do not go beyond what is given in experience, but rather because the inferences needed to establish them involve only very general assumptions shared by all speakers of the language.

To the obvious rejoinder that the dismissal of data sentences leaves nothing for cognition to process, the answer is that, at the lowest level – the level which produces observational judgements – cognition works upon purely physical inputs to the brain, and thus below the "language threshold" at which inputs are encoded in symbolic, linguistic form.[4] What creates trouble for intercultural translation is the fact that this cognitive processing is in part, and indirectly, shaped by those higher-order, culturally determined beliefs in which civilizations typically differ. These divergent beliefs (theories) contribute to the sense of the sentences in which they are expressed, and thus make translation impossible across cultural barriers.

However, in order to examine this reasoning, it is necessary to formulate it more carefully on the basis of some plausible, explicit theory of meaning. Unfortunately, this leads us straight into one of the most controversial areas of philosophy, with nothing by way of a received opinion for us to lean against. In particular, the Argument from Theory Loading, as I shall dub the above reasoning (or for short the ATL) may be expected to come out differently when built upon a realist and an anti-realist theory of meaning, respectively, in the sense that Dummett has given to these terms. This is not the place to try to adjudicate the battle between realism and anti-realism in philosophy of language, and to decide on a single conception of meaning upon which to base our subsequent reasoning, desirable as this procedure would be. Instead, I shall adopt the strategy of dividing my discussion into two parts, each corresponding to one of the major rival conceptions of meaning.

Still, there is a general conception of meaning in terms of which we may render the ATL more precise before we look at the special features of its realist and anti-realist versions. According to this conception, which embodies a moderate holism and which has been critically examined by Dummett[5], the meaning of a term is its contribution to fixing the sense of the sentences in which it occurs; the sense of a sentence is its contribution to fixing the truth conditions – whether realistically or anti-realistically conceived – of the total set of sentences of the language. The channels through which the semantic determination flows are the inferential ties between sentences, by virtue of which the assignment of a particular truth value to one sentence will have repercussions on the truth values assigned to other sentences. In the realist case, these will be deductive ties, in the antirealist case, they may also comprise weaker, non-deductive ties, if the anti-realist position in question is defined not in terms of verification conditions, but in terms of some weaker notion of evidential support.[6]

When construed in terms of this holist conception of meaning, the ATL comes out as follows: Any sentence expressing a belief generally entertained within a culture (a "theory") will possess inferential connections to other sentences of that culture's language, thereby generating inferential ties between those sentences that would not exist in the absence of that belief. Different beliefs establish different connections which, through the overall network of interrelated sentences which constitutes the culture's "world view", affect every single sentence of the language. It follows that no sentence of the alien language can have the same sense as a sentence in the anthropologist's or the historian's language. For the sense of a sentence, on the above characterization, is a function of its location in the network of inferential connections, and these networks are never identical across cultures, since each of them will contain nodes – consisting in sentences expressing beliefs unique to the particular culture – which have no counterpart in any other network. As the overall networks are never identical, neither do they contain perfectly identical locations, as defined in terms of their relations to other nodes in the network.

Before we proceed, we must dispose of a suspicion that the theory of meaning suggested here – of which I have provided only the merest outline – is not neutral between a realist and an anti-realist reading, but actually excludes the former: On a realist conception, it might be said, truth conditions are ascribed to sentences in isolation, as their individual property. Our moderately holistic theory of meaning, on the other hand, construes the overall theories of which sentences are the constituents as the only autonomous bearers of truth conditions, leaving to individual sentences the task of contributing to the determination of those conditions. Indeed the idea of the sense of a sentence as its *contribution* to a global assignment of truth conditions has its home in the anti-realist conception and does not transfer to the realist version at all. (Historically, the idea was of course developed by Quine in "Two Dogmas of Empiricism", as a part of a reformed verificationist theory of meaning).

Yet this objection is mistaken. It is true that on a realist view, fewer inferential ties between sentences will count as meaning-conferring, since a large proportion will be construed as merely providing evidence for the truth of the sentences to which they are linked, while contributing nothing to the sense of those sentences. As a matter of fact, this will hold for all non-deductive ties. But the fact remains, of course, that even on a realist view, there are inferential connections between sentences, even beyond those of formal logic, by virtue of explicit or implicit interdefinition of terms. Thanks to the definitional ties between the core concepts of our conceptual system and its more peripheral elements, the theoretical loading of the former will spread to the entire vocabulary. Thus, for instance, it might be said that our modern conception of material objects is essentially – by implicit definition – that of an inanimate entity, whereas the corresponding primitive concept is of things as active, volitional beings. This difference, which will affect the rest of the vocabulary, survives on a realist interpretation of meaning.

V

The ATL as I have stated it so far agrees with standard presentation in neglecting an important distinction, thereby gaining some illicit power. This is the distinction between a theory as the sum total of the speakers' beliefs (call this conception "theory$_1$", and a theory as a body of interrelated propositions with which the speakers are familiar, but to which they do not necessarily give any credence (call this "theory$_2$". Notice that theories$_1$ form a proper subset of theories$_2$). Now that in which a sophisticated and a primitive culture will typically differ is theory$_1$, i.e. beliefs; however, it is differences in theory$_2$ which are responsible for differences in meaning. A theory with which I am familiar, but which I reject, will still determine the sense of the sentences I use to state that theory.

Appreciation of this distinction makes us realize that the representatives of two different cultures may endorse radically different theories, and their languages still be intertranslatable, since they are conversant with the same set of theories$_2$. This is not merely a remote theoretical possibility: The anthropologist's efforts to understand contemporary natives is greatly aided by the preservation, in his language, of ancient belief systems encapsulated in semantic relics. The natives' talk of occult agencies responsible for various kinds of mischief can be translated into talk about "witches" and "evil spirits", since these terms are part of a theory which lives on in the linguistic heritage of the anthropologist's culture although no longer being endorsed. The doxastic standing of these terms has no bearing upon their usefulness in translating the natives' utterances.

In drawing the distinction between the grasp of a given term and the endorsement of its applicability, we have to concede, of course, that the former must go beyond mere possession, on the anthropologist's part, of a record of the occasions on which the natives have previously used that term: The anthropologist must be able to *project* that record, applying the term to novel situations which were not in the original corpus. But it is wrong to maintain, as has sometimes been done, that this ability amounts to an endorsement of the native concept, or to the subscription to native beliefs.[7] There is no more warrant for saying that the anthropologist must endorse native beliefs in order to understand them than there is for saying that the logician who champions classical logic must still somehow endorse the intuitionist logic to which he is ostensibly opposed, if we are to grant that he understands that logic at all. What is required is merely that he be capable of operating with intuitionist logic.

However, the ATL can be upheld in the face of the distinction between theory$_1$ and theory$_2$ if we invoke the concept of topics that are *inaccessible* to a given culture, whether as objects of belief or of mere comprehension. Obviously, the cognitive differences between cultures do not consist merely in the fact that they distribute truth values differently across identical total sets of propositions, i.e. theories$_2$: Any culture will entertain beliefs that are *inaccessible* to other cultures. The notion of inaccessible theories, or beliefs, directs attention away from the nodes in the theoretical network and towards the inferential links between them: To say that a belief is inaccessible to a given culture is to say that it is etablished by means of rules of inference which that culture would reject as invalid, and which are no part of its intellectual heritage, either. In other words, certain beliefs will be inaccessible to a given culture because the inferential avenues which lead to them do not stand open to that culture.

Adopting this notion, the modified version of the ATL will claim that any culture will subscribe to certain beliefs that are inaccessible to other cultures and are hence untranslatable into their languages, since those beliefs occupy nodes in the inferential framework of language which have no counterpart in the other idioms. A concrete example of such deviant modes of reasoning might be the native culture's reliance upon oracles to ascertain the presence of certain properties in human beings, in a manner with which the anthropologist is not familiar from his own cultural inheritance and which contravenes the rules of evidence to which he is accustomed. A famous and oft-quoted case is found in Evans-Pritchard's puzzled and puzzling account of the bird oracle and its role in the life of the Azande people of the Sudan.[8] In conducting their everyday business, the Azande rely heavily upon information obtained through the bird oracle. In a secretive ceremony heavily surrounded by ritual, a fowl is fed a poison in a dose which is not invariably lethal; the death or survival of the bird is then taken as constituting a positive or negative answer to questions which the agent poses subsequent to administration of the poison. The questions are typically aimed at discovering future threats to the agent's life or well-being, contingent upon different lines of action on his part, and the ways to avoid them. The oracle's verdict is taken as authoritative; or rather, the institution recognizes different levels of authority and dependability. At the top is the king's oracle, which is accorded final authority.

The logic of this institution is radically different from modern Western ways of thinking, and has no counterpart, at least to any degree of detail, in ancient strata of our modern languages. And this difference in reasoning leads to a difference in the meanings of the terms involved: The evidential ties between a certain outcome of the bird oracle and a certain property of a person – say, his being causally responsible for some accident – has an impact upon the content of the corresponding concept, *in casu* the native notion of causal agency: The report that a person brought about a certain outcome has a different sense in the native language than in ours, since it can be established, and refuted, by means which seem to us to have no bearing upon that question at all; or at least so the proponent of the ATL will argue.

VI

In illustrating the strengthened version of the ATL by the example of the bird oracle above, we tacitly adopted an antirealist reading of that argument: We talked about the meaning of a sentence as being a function of the *evidence* which favours or disfavours it. However, the improved version af the ATL, and with it the notion of a belief which is inaccessible to the members of a given culture, can be given a realist reading, too. According to a realist view, linguistic competence depends upon an arsenal of projective devices used to link sentences, the meaning of which transcends experience, to their epistemically inaccessible truth conditions. One such link is provided by the analogical reasoning which persuades me that people enjoy the same private mental states as I do when they behave in a similar manner. Another is at play when I grasp the truth conditions of past sentences by considering the truth conditions of their present tensed versions and then imaginatively shift those conditions backwards along the time axis, as it were.

Now in his realist guise, the champion of the ATL will argue that any culture will endorse beliefs that are inaccessible to other cultures, because the projections employed to fix the content of transcendent beliefs differ from one culture to another: Different cultures adopt divergent ways of extending truth conditions into the transcendent realm, making for translation-defying differences of meaning between the transcendent sentences of those languages. For instance, many primitive peoples take the causal potency of certain substances as a sign that they embody a certain active something-or-other the nature of which is not exhausted by that causal potency, and which thus transcends experience; an inference which we do not share in our culture. This difference would thus seem to generate intranslatability between the two languages.

This argument, if sound, only goes to show that certain specified sentences of the native language are resistant to translation. For a realist theory of semantics will not claim that all sentences possess transcendent truth conditions. But here the champion of the ATL will once again invoke the modest holism upon which that argument is premised to demonstrate that the local differences in meaning will be transmitted to the entire language: Linguistic terms being pervasively interdefined, a difference in one corner of the network will have global repercussions that are conducted by these interconnections.

VII

It is time to assess the merits of the argument I have sketched in support of the Hermetic Thesis in its translational version. Basically, there are two ways in which that reasoning might be impugned. One is to assail the ATL and the semantic conception on which it is based, the other is to show that this conception, even if valid, does not have detrimental implications for translation. We start with a criticism of the former kind, borrowed from the debate concerning incommensurability of scientific theories across paradigms which shows striking parallels to the topic we are concerned with here.

To assert that theories are incommensurable is to assert, *inter alia*, that the sentences of which those theories consist are not intertranslatable. And the grounds on which incommensurability has been upheld in natural science derive precisely from the fact that the sense of theoretical sentences is a function of the total theory of which they form a part. Hence, theories which diverge in their core axioms – and especially if the difference is one involving different paradigms – bring with them a difference in the languages in which they are couched: The languages will not be intertranslatable.[9]

This reasoning has been opposed by Putnam, and others.[10] Their criticism is based upon the semantics for natural kind terms proposed by Putnam and Kripke. According to this semantics, natural kind terms of the type occurring in physical theories are not defined by those theories; instead, such terms are associated with a vague and highly revisable cluster of observational notions which serve to single out the terms' extensions, in actual and possible worlds. The expression "single out" is crucial: It indicates that in this semantic theory, natural kind terms are not *defined* by the associated observational notions, in the manner of a definite description. Rather, the observational specification serves as an instruction, as it were, for singling out the extension, a guide that helps us pin it down.[11]

Given this semantic theory, the prospects for translation across scientific paradigms improve dramatically. As long as the same physical kind is singled out by two terms, i.e. as long as their extensions are the same, even in possible worlds, the two terms will translate each other. It does not matter if the recipes for singling out the extensions are not the same, since they are not a part of the meaning of the terms.

I would go along with this counter to the ATL part of the way. However, I believe that it needs some qualification when applied to the anthropological and historical case, which substantially weakens its power to resolve our present predicament. Although it is true that natural kind terms do not possess a meaning which reflects the fine details of the theories in which they occur, it remains a fact that their use is governed by more general features of those theories. For instance, it is part of the meaning of the natural kind terms introduced by modern physics that the entities to which they refer are inanimate. (This is not to say that they are explicitly thus defined within physical theory, but rather implicitly in the everyday language which has adopted the physical term). If it turned out that the effects we attribute to electrons were due to entities that are not merely quite different from what we have taken electrons to be so far, but are actually little creatures endowed with intelligence and will, we should cease to refer to these items as "electrons", or at least concede that the term had undergone a change of meaning. Conversely, to take an example from anthropology, if the natives believe that (what we call) epileptic seizures are cases of demon possession, it will not do to translate their term for this phenomenon by "epileptic seizure", since the native term is naturally taken to involve an ontology of personalized entities, whereas our term points to an aetiology of purely physiological factors. The native term rules out that the description of the "essential nature" of that which causes epileptic seizures can be given in purely physiological terms, while our notion assumes precisely this.[12]

For this reason, the argument against the ATL is less successful in anthropology than in the debate concerning incommensurability in natural science. The latter takes place within a purely materialist framework such that anti-spiritualist implications of physical terms do not create a divide between rival descriptions. In the anthropological and historical case, such major differences will often be involved. Hence the ATL still has some force here: Although we have rejected the idea that a linguistic term is defined by the theory (the total set of beliefs) which it serves to express, it would still seem that certain general aspects of the theory will be reflected in the meaning of the term.

Another worry about the usefulness of the Putnam-Kripke argument for our present problem is that it deals with natural kind terms only, leaving the ATL free to threaten translation of other categories of terms, such as names of artifacts, social roles, institutions, psychological characteristics, and others. Some of these phenomena are quite central in the life of the people studied and will have to occupy a prominent place in the anthropologist's or historian's efforts at translation.

VIII

The attempt to rebut the Hermetic Thesis by undermining the doctrine of theory loading thus ends in failure. Instead, we must try the other angle, assessing whether theory loading really constitutes a bar to translation in the sense we have adopted here. At this juncture, we must again address the realist and anti-realist versions of the ATL separately.

In the anti-realist version of the argument, it would seem that the ATL is not powerful enough to block translation. Recall that our notion of translation is that of a verbal means of conveying the semantically relevant features of the term or sentence to be translated. There is no requirement that this be achieved by aligning *quoted* expressions in the anthropologist's or historian's language with *quoted* expressions in the native language: The translator is permitted to *use* his own language to describe the way the alien language is used, drawing freely in the process upon a semantic metalanguage that is not a part of the expressions that are glossed.

More specifically, this approach allows the translator to *state* those inferential ties between sentences which are not accepted or otherwise available in his own culture, in this way rendering the sense even of sentences which express inaccessible beliefs. He does this by indicating the closest equivalent in his own language to the native sentence to be rendered, proceeding then to state the aberrant inferential ties which exist between this sentence and other sentences in the native language, again represented by their closest equivalents in his own language. For instance, if the natives, under certain specified conditions, take oracular verdicts to provide overriding evidence that a certain person caused an accident, even against the kind of empirical evidence that is normally accepted as rebutting such a charge, we can provide an account of this divergent notion of causal agency by describing the occult evidence and its evidential power vis-a-vis the empirical evidence. This account will not possess the same meaning as a native sentence attributing causal agency, since it belongs to a metalevel relative to that sentence; no sentence is semantically equivalent to its own metalinguistic description of the kind involved here. Moreover, no single word used in the account will be equivalent to the native term for causal agency. Still, that account will tell us everything there is to know about the meaning of that term.

But why can it not be granted that the native term actually *means* the same as the statement, in our language, of the disjunctive set of its satisfaction conditions, i.e. something like "... is tied to another type of event by relations of regular succession, contiguity, etc. [i.e., *our* criteria of causality] *or* evokes such-and-such a response from the oracle"? But this gloss fails to reveal that the natives take this disjunction to represent a unified concept, in which the second disjunct overrides the first as a criterion of causal agency in certain settings: In those cases in which questions about causal agency may be appealed to the oracle – which may not be all cases – a conflict between the oracle's verdict and the empirical evidence will be taken to mean that the latter is non-veridical; i.e. that a mistake was made in the description of that evidence. The relation between the two types of criteria for causal agency is thus not the same as the relation between the components of an ordinary multicriterial concept. We might for instance introduce a multicriterial concept of death, for medical purposes, for which the criteria would be the absence of heart activity, or the absence of brain activity, or the absence of both. But we would not take the observation that heart activity was present to entail the non-veridicality of an observation to the effect that brain activity had ceased, or vice versa: The two criteria are independent and do not exert evidential pressure upon each other. The native criteria of causal agency, on the other hand, exert such pressure, a circumstance that cannot be captured in an object-language use of the anthropologist's idiom, since it lacks the corresponding inferential links. Such links can only be conveyed in a metalinguistic account, in which the anthropologist's language is used to *state* the inferential connections in the native language.

But, it might be said, does a conflict between the empirical evidence and the occult evidence, resolved in favour of the latter, not force the natives to redescribe the former in a more basic, observational language? Will they not have to admit that in reporting the empirical evidence, they went beyond the bare data and imposed an interpretation upon it; an unwarranted one, as it later turned out? And will the language in which these bare data are subsequently described not be one which the natives share with the anthropologist, thus overcoming intranslatability? At least this observational language will not be contaminated by the natives' aberrant inferential habits, since native patterns of inference are defined over that very language which they hence presuppose as a prior, independent foundation.

But this reasoning fails. The phenomenal language to which the natives may resort when empirical evidence is overridden by the oracle will typically be parasitic upon the language in which that evidence was originally reported. The natives will say things like, "The two events *appeared* to be correlated in such-and-such a manner [e.g., the manner which ordinarily justifies the conclusion that one causes the other]; but the oracle tells us that they were not". This report employs the native vocabulary, replete with its aberrant inferential links, and hence remains untranslatable into the anthropologist's idiom; the fact that these terms are embedded within an "appearance"-operator makes no difference. For the critic's point to go through, the language on which the natives fall back in case of conflict between criteria would have to be a pure observational language which made no semantic loans from the rest of the language. But it is by now a commonplace in philosophy that such a pristine idiom is not available to any culture. (It might be thought that all that is needed for translatability to be saved is for the native observational language to make the *same* loans as the anthropologist's. However, the present argument is premised upon a holist conception of language. Hence, if the native observational language were tainted by a part of the more theoretical strata of language, it would be tainted by the whole of it).

IX

The procedure for rendering native meanings which I outlined above turns the argument for intranslatability against itself. The argument claimed that differences in the inferential connections between sentences of the native language and the home language render translation of native sentences impossible. But if there is a determinate fact of the matter as to which inferences the natives use and which inferences are employed in the anthropologist's culture, it must be possible to identify those divergent canons of inference and thereby specify the semantic differences which distinguish the two languages; i.e. it must be possible in this way to specify the meaning of native terms and sentences. This possibility is guaranteed by a premise which we are entitled to use, at least on an *ad hominem* basis, at the present stage where we examine the anti-realist version of the Hermetic Thesis: This is the premise that the deviant inferential habits of the natives must be fully manifested in their behaviour, and hence fully recordable by the anthropologist. If differences in meaning are indeed a function of differences in inferential principles, we shall have captured these differences when we have spelled out the divergent inferences of the native language, and have singled out those inferences in our language which the natives hold invalid.

It is true that the description of these inferential ties will be couched in *our* language with its distinctive semantics; but this creates no problem, since these descriptions are not required to be semantically equivalent to any set of sentences in the object language, but merely to *state* every semantically relevant feature of those sentences. It is also true that the sentences which such accounts cite as being inferentially tied to the target sentences are only the closest counterparts in the metalanguage to the relevant sentences in the object language, not their exact equivalents. However, the same procedure will be applied to these sentences in their turn, specifying the inferential connections which set them apart from their counterparts in the metalanguage. If the Argument from Theory Loading is indeed right in assuming that the differences between the anthropologist's language and the native language are due to differences in inferential canons, and if we are now entitled to the anti-realist premise that such canons must be capable of manifestation in speech behaviour, it must be possible to capture the semantic divergencies by tracing out the network of inferential connections, slowly and by degrees. This procedure may well lead to highly complicated glosses of native terms; but in principle it must be possible to achieve a full picture of the semantics of the native language in this way.

It might be objected that this saddles the anthropologist with a task that is not so much immense as actually infinite, given that native sentences are an infinite lot. For this makes the network of inferential interconnections to be traced out a unbounded one. In response, we may point out that the inferential ties between sentences must be governed by certain general principles which are finitely statable. If not, the native language becomes perniciously holistic in a manner which makes it impossible to learn, not only for the anthropologist but for the natives as well. It is a commonplace that language is projectible in such a way that speakers will utter, and comprehend, sentences which they have never heard before; in learning a language, the speaker achieves the ability to grasp a potential infinitude of sentences. This is only possible if, corresponding to the finite number of ways in which expressions are constructed out of simpler expressions, there is a finite number of ways in which the meanings of sentences are derived from the meanings of the terms of which they are composed, and from their syntactic form. There could be no such finite procedure of interpretation, on anti-realist premises, if the evidential relations between sentences did not obey certain general and finitely statable principles. In spelling out these principles, the anthropologist only faces a finite task.

X

We have disposed of the most popular argument in favour of intranslatability. But obviously, the defeat of that argument only brings the defeat of the intranslatability view with it if differences in inferential patterns are the only plausible source of meaning variance between languages.

I shall briefly examine one other possible source. While the previous argument focussed upon interrelations among sentences, the present one focusses upon the relation between sentences and the world. I.e., it focusses upon those sentences the meaning of which is to a significant degree fixed through the association of the sentences with certain directly observable states of affairs. It must be kept in mind, however, that on the present view, no sentences are observational in the sense of dealing with "raw sense data", but only in the sense that speakers will reach a consensus about their truth value on the basis of mere observation of the world, regardless of background information.

The argument would be that the native population enjoys certain kinds of sensations and experiences, with which the translator is not familiar. These might range from simple experiences of the taste and smell of local foodstuffs, to such subtle items as mystic experiences, associated e.g. with indigenous religious practices. These two extreme cases call for different treatment in relation to the translatability issue.

Would the presence in the native language of terms for sensory qualities unknown in the translator's culture render that language untranslatable? Presumably, the answer is yes on a standard, narrow reading of the word "translation". For instance, the highly developed gustatory vocabulary of French wine-waiters would be untranslatable to an anthropologist from a culture in which wines were unknown. However, we decided initially to diverge from standard understanding of the word "translation" if it suited our purposes, i.e., in case failure of translation would constitute no embarrasment to an anthropologist or historian. And here it would generally be felt that failure to achieve translation of simple sensory terms does not constitute a problem, at least so long as the translating language has the means to single out those items that produce the unique sensory qualities, and so long as the translating language possesses the general category of the experiential terms in question, e.g. names for gustatory qualities. Such a shortcoming would be accidental, much like a difference in the stocks of proper names available to two languages, and could be remedied by the simple addition of a suitable term.

The case of terms used to report mystic experiences associated with religious ceremonies, trances, etc. poses larger problems. It is not very plausible to say that a failure to translate such terms would be trivial, if e.g. the experiences in question were taken to be cases of direct experiential contact with supernatural forces or deities. Not only will such entities be of great importance in the culture in question; moreover, the shortcoming can not be remedied by the simple addition of terms, since it is not clear that the translator's language has slots reserved for this kind of term, as it were. (Religious mystics typically claim that their experiences cannot be expressed in the ordinary language. Their complaint evidently is not that it is impossible to invent new words to tag those experiences).

Still, this threat to translatability may be sidestepped on the grounds that what we are dealing with here are not strictly speaking *experiences*, in the sense of objects of observational report. For the sentences describing them are not likely to command general assent across cultures, but presuppose immersion in a particular culture. They express a particular, highly theoretical interpretation of a core of experiences (an interpretation, moreover, which is definitely above the "language threshold" mentioned earlier). This is precisely the reason why they cannot be incorporated into the translator's language by the simple expedient of inventing a name for them. Hence, the divergencies of meaning spring from differences in theoretical links between sentences, differences in inferential pattern. In other words, the present challenge to translatability turns out to be of the same kind that we examined previously. Hence the conclusion of that examination must hold for the present case too, viz. that semantic differences springing from divergent inferential habits pose no problem for translation, given that an anti-realist construal of language use is adopted.

These remarks do not suffice to establish the translatability view, even in its anti-realist reading. For there is no guarantee that we have exhausted the sources of radical meaning variance. But they place the burden of proof on the shoulders of one opposing that view. They saddle him with the task of finding other sources of intranslatability than differences in inferential patterns, or differences in experiences.

XI

Turning now to the realist version of the ATL, we recognize that it cannot be disposed of by means of the argument which proved effective against the anti-realist version. Our rebuttal of this argument depended upon a premise peculiar to the anti-realist view, namely that the natives' aberrant inferential practices are open to observation and may hence be recorded in our language (although only a *complete* description of native habits of inference will suffice to capture the precise content of *any* native canon of reasoning). The realist version denies that native patterns of reasoning will always be thus open; this is a corollary to the tenet that some of these patterns extend to topics that are not themselves observationally accessible.

According to the realist view, the native language resists translation because it embodies different truth value projections than those used in the anthropologist's language. The anthropologist cannot specify these projections in his own language, not even when used as a metalanguage, since to do so he would have to describe those inaccessible states of affairs with which the native projections establish referential contact. But *ex hypothesi* his language fails to connect with those states.

However, on its realist reading, the Argument from Theory Loading is not yet complete. To lay claim to our attention, it must show in a positive manner that translation will fail: A demonstration that failure of translation is a logical possibility commands little interest. (However, such a demonstration is convenient in showing that translation is not guaranteed everywhere, and thus that the notion of "translation" adopted here does not trivialize the issue). But so far only a possibility proof has been offered, since no positive grounds have been given that alien cultures actually adopt different canons of truth condition projection. To raise the modal strength of the conclusion, it must for instance be shown that the natives take certain facts to point beyond themselves to an epistemically inaccessible realm, where we see no such implication. Unfortunately, the demonstration of such a divergence does not definitively establish the desired conclusion: Although the native projection rule is demonstrably different, that which is projected may still be available within our language. To take an example we used previously: many primitive peoples take the causal potency of certain substances as a sign that they embody a certain active something-or-other which transcends experience, an inference which we reject. However, what is attributed may well be the same as that which we ascribe to our fellow human beings in using such words as "will", "intelligence", "mind", etc. The difference in projective habits would not generate intranslatability in this case.

Perhaps there is actually a way for a proponent of the Hermetic Thesis to strengthen his position. Remember that he only disputes the *translatability* of the native language, not that the anthropologist may *learn* it. So he is allowed to make play with the possibility that the anthropologist might acquire a grasp of the native language and discover that he had picked up novel ways of projecting truth conditions in the process. Or the anthropologist might interview "natural" bilinguals as to whether the native part of their personalities uses different projections than the Westernized part. Pending the presentation of such – rather obscure – evidence, the realist version of the ATL is incomplete, and the onus is upon the proponent of the Hermetic Thesis to strengthen his position if we are to get seriously involved with it. True, in the nature of the case, we cannot ask him to produce conclusive evidence that the natives use divergent canons of projection; for it is definitory of the current version of the Hermetic Thesis that these canons are not fully manifested in native behaviour, or in any other observable data. Still, it is incumbent upon the proponent of the Hermetic Thesis to provide us with plausible grounds, lest his position reduce to idle speculation.

The champion of intranslatability has a final option, of course: He may make a sceptical turn, urging that the crucial issue is not whether we have positive grounds for believing that the natives employ different projections, but that we can never know for sure that they do not. Yet this move backfires: It brings us face to face with a problem that crops up in intracultural "translation", too, i.e. in the way I map the sentences I utter onto those uttered by the other speakers of my language (syntactically defined). The sceptical argument starts every one of us wondering whether he uses language with the same meanings as his associates. Thus, in taking the sceptical turn, we shall have wound up with an instance of the general problem of other minds, leaving behind the narrower problem about obstacles to translation produced by cultural differences which we set out to investigate.

Notes
My research for the present article was supported by a grant from the Carlsberg Foundation; I would like to express my gratitude to this institution. Jens Ravnkilde and Peter Sandøe provided helpful criticisms of an earlier draft.

1. The classical statement of this position within anthropology is found in various of the articles collected in Lee Whorf, Benjamin (1956) *Language, Thought and Reality* (New York, Wiley).
2. As an example of this kind of opposed but identically based positions, see Malpas, J.E. (1989) "The Intertranslatability of Natural Languages", *Synthese* 78, pp. 233-64, who comes out in favour of translatability, and Jennings, Richard C. (1988) "Translation, Interpretation and Understanding", *Philosophy of the Social Sciences* 18 (1988,) who comes out against it.
3. Davidson, Donald (1973) "On the Very Idea of a Conceptual Scheme", *Proceedings and Addresses of the American Philosophical Association* 47 (1973-74), pp. 5-20.
4. Such radicals as Jerry Fodor maintain that even brain processes make use of a system of representation, a language cf.; *The Language of Thought* (Hassocks: The Harvester Press, 1976). But even if we grant this – which I would be reluctant to do – this does not undermine the point I am making here, which is simply that the public, common language that the anthropologist is concerned with can fail to comprise data sentences. This argument is not impugned by the possibility that the brain conducts a silent soliloquy in a private language comprising, *inter alia*, pure data sentences.

5. See for instance *Frege: Philosophy of Language* (London: Duckworth, 1973), chapter 17. In this chapter Dummett is concerned, *inter alia*, to distinguish the moderate holism of this theory from another, more radical kind.
6. Such a version af anti-realism is embraced by Dummett in the Preface to *Truth and Other Enigmas* (London: Duckworth, 1978), and in the article "Realism" reprinted in that volume.
7. For a recent example, see Papineau, David (1979) *Theory and Meaning* (Oxford: Clarendon Press), p. 75 f. Apart from this point, I find much to agree with in Papineau's discussion of radical translation.
8. In *Witchcraft, Oracles and Magic among the Azande* (Oxford: Clarendon Press, 1937), part III.
9. An excellent exposition of the incommensurability argument is found in Newton-Smith, W.H. (1981) *The Rationality of Science* (London, Routledge & Kegan Paul), chapter VII.
10. Cf. Putnam, Hilary (1975) "What is "Realism"?", *Aristotelian Society Proceedings* LXXVI (1975-76), pp. 177-94. Putnam's argument is elaborated upon by W.H. Newton-Smith in *The Rationality of Science*, chapter VII.
11. The referential semantics for natural kind terms is presented in a number of not entirely equivalent formulations in the works of Putnam and Kripke; see e.g. Putnam, Hilary (1975) "The meaning of "meaning"", in K. Gunderson (ed.), *Language, Mind and Knowledge. Minnesota Studies in the Philosophy of Science* VII. (Minneapolis, University of Minnesota Press, 1975), and Kripke, Saul (1972) "Naming and Necessity", in Donald Davidson & Gilbert Harman (eds.), *Semantics Of Natural Language*. (Dordrecht, D. Reidel Publishing Company, 1972). The version of referential semantics I sketch out here comprises what seem to me the most plausible elements. It moreover bypasses the thorny question concerning the role af causality in reference.
12. For a somewhat similar point, made with reference to the debate over incommensurability in natural science, see David Papineau, *Theory and Meaning*, pp. 156-68.

POPULATION ETHICS
On Parfit's Views Concerning Future Generations

W. ROBERT PULVERTAFT

University of Copenhagen

I

Suppose we are going to choose between two different policies for the development of the size of a population. The first one, Replacement, means encouraging (e.g. economically) people to have only two children per couple. The second one, Growth, means encouraging people to have more than two children per couple until the size of the population has reached a certain level. This will probably take about six generations; after that we shall try to keep the size of the population constant. Let us assume that if we choose Replacement, the quality of life will steadily increase. If we choose Growth, the quality of life will steadily increase for the first four generations. In the next two generations the quality of life will fall (because of limited resources). After that the people will become steadily better off again (because of the development of alternatives to traditional resources). The different developments can be shown as in fig. 1.

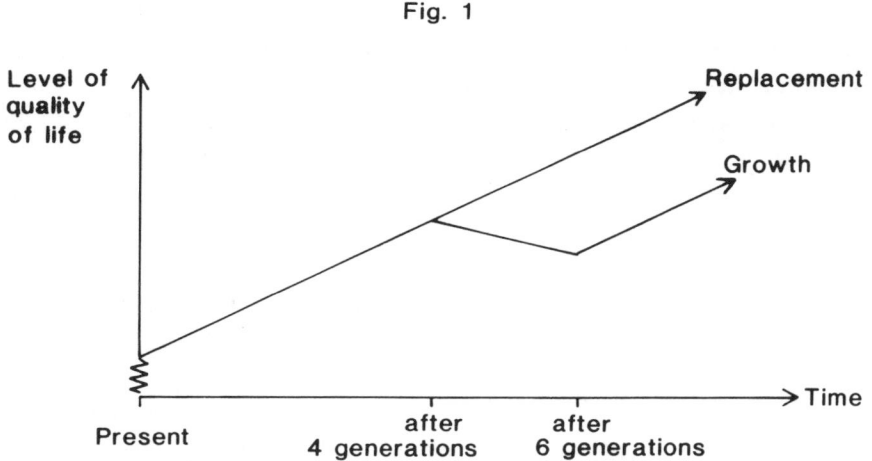

Fig. 1

Let us also assume that it will always be so that at a certain time everybody will be equally well off. The alternatives after six generations can be shown as in fig. 2.

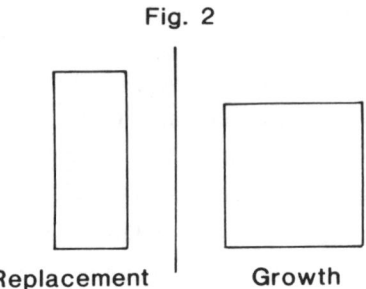

Fig. 2

Replacement   Growth

The width of the blocks shows the number of people living, the height shows how high the quality of these people's lives is.

I believe that even if one does not assume cardinality in the scale of quality of life the two figures provide an acceptable illustration of the alternatives.

If we choose Replacement the level of the quality of life will be higher after six generations, whereas the quantity of happiness and suffering will be smaller, (suffering having of course negative value). If we choose Growth the quantity of happiness and suffering will be larger after six generations, while the level of the quality of life will be lower. This will of course also apply to the alternative populations farther on in the future.

Most of us believe the following: If a person had not grown from a pair of cells with at least one cell in common with the pair of cells he/she did actually grow from, he/she would in fact not have existed. Given this claim we will assume that all the people that live after four generations will be different depending on which policy we choose. (People would find different partners, and couples would have children at different times).

Which policy should we choose?

(The above example is very much inspired by the examples "Depletion" and "the Down Escalator Case" from: Parfit, Derek (1984) *Reasons and Persons* (Oxford, Oxford University Press), p. 362 and 382).

All theories of normative ethics include the view that when we make a moral judgement of an act we must among other things judge the consequences of this act, and that the consequential happiness and suffering are important for the moral judgement. When we judge the consequences of a particular possible act – outcome (a) – as being worse than the consequences of another act – outcome (b) – it is normally with reference to it being worse *for someone* if outcome (a) rather than outcome (b) came about.

The reason why this is normally applicable to judgements of the consequences of acts is that in the different possible outcomes of our possible acts we are normally dealing with *the same people*. But when we judge acts – such as the choice between Replacement and Growth – that determine which people shall live this is not the case. When we judge the consequences of these acts we must compare outcomes in which different people live, and sometimes, as in this case, also outcomes where a different number of people live.

In order to compare outcomes where a different number of people live we must have a solution to the following problem which I will call

> the *Problem of Beneficence*: What are the relative moral values of 1: the quantity of happiness and suffering and 2: the level of the quality of life?

In part four of his book *Reasons and Persons* Derek Parfit addresses the Problem of Beneficence, but he does not find it solvable. It is not my aim to provide a solution, but rather to raise some points that Parfit seems to have overlooked.

The first and longest part of this paper will be a critical account of Parfit's discussions. After that I will examine an alternative solution to the Problem of Beneficence which is very similar to one of the solutions discussed by Parfit, but which does not lead to the unacceptable conclusions that are the corollary of these. Finally I will explain why I do not believe this alternative to be the right solution.

Before proceeding some definitions will be stated:

1) Moral value: The moral value is the value we give something when making a moral judgement of it. In this paper we shall only be concerned with the moral value of outcomes. When I use the term "value" and nothing else is stated, it will be in the sense of moral value.

2) Personal value: The personal value is the value something has to a person.

3) Happiness: The term "happiness" will in this paper mean "whatever has positive personal value".
4) Suffering: The term "suffering" will for present purposes mean "whatever has negative personal value".
5) Quantity has value: The phrase "quantity has value" will be used to mean that in the moral judgement of an outcome the quantity of happiness and suffering in this outcome is of importance.
6) Quality has value: The phrase "quality has value" will in this paper mean that in the moral judgement of an outcome the level of the quality of life in this outcome is of importance.
7) Happiness and suffering have quantitative value: When quantity has value, happiness and suffering have value in so far as they contribute positively or negatively to the total quantity of happiness minus suffering. Therefore I will also phrase "quantity has value" as "happiness and suffering have quantitative value".

Two comments should be made on the last proposition: a) When I say that happiness and suffering have value, I use the word "value" in the sense of both positive and negative value; b) I do not presume cardinality in the scale of quality of life. The word "minus" only assumes that we can make a total estimation of the quantity of happiness and the quantity of suffering, and that this estimation involves some kind of subtraction. (The concept of quantitative value is not used by Parfit, but in my opinion it is a very useful concept in the discussion of the Problem of Beneficence.)

With the definitions above we can restate the Problem of Beneficence as:
What are the relative values of quantity and quality?

II

There are two groups of principles that lay down guidelines for the solution of the Problem of Beneficence. These principles can be divided into the two groups according to their answer to the following question: If in one of two outcomes the people living would be less happy, can this always be morally outweighed by a sufficient increase in the quantity of happiness? In other words: Can a decrease in quality always be morally outweighed by an increase in quantity?

An answer in the affirmative will, as we see, also be an acceptance of what Parfit calls

> the *Repugnant Conclusion*: For any possible population, no matter how large it is or how high the quality of the life in it is, there must be some other possible population in which everybody has a life that is only barely worth living, which, other things being equal, would be better if only this latter population is large enough.

As the name indicates Parfit cannot accept this conclusion.

Two principles give an answer in the affirmative to the above question. The first one, which we will call the Total Principle, says:

(1) Only quantity has value, i.e.: Happiness and suffering have only quantitative value – in the following way: The only thing of value is the total quantity of happiness minus suffering. Quality has no value.

The second principle that gives an answer in the affirmative to the question asked is:

(2) Quantity has value, i.e.: Happiness and suffering have quantitative value. Quality has also value.

Now let us look at the principles involved in a negative answer, that is to say a decrease in quality cannot always be outweighed by an increase in quantity. At the extreme there is the Average Principle:

(3) Quantity has no value, i.e.: Happiness and suffering have no quantitative value. Only quality has value – in the following way: The only thing of value is the average amount of happiness minus suffering.

For well known reasons we must reject this principle, and maintain that quantity does have value, or in other words that happiness and suffering have quantitative value.

One way to avoid the Repugnant Conclusion, if one is of the opinion that happiness and suffering have quantitative value, is to fix an upper limit to this quantitative value of happiness and suffering. The most plausible of the two principles formulated by Parfit that incorporate this proposal is:

(4) Quantity has value, i. e.: Happiness and suffering have quantitative value – in the following way: The quantitative value of happiness and suffering during any period has an upper limit. As the actual quantity of happiness and suffering increases, the quantitative value of extra happiness and suffering declines and asymptotically approaches zero. Quality has value, – in the following way: When the level of the quality of life is higher, there is a higher upper limit to the quantitative value of happiness and suffering during any period.

This principle can be extended to say that quality has value in the sense that it is bad if the level of the quality of life is lower than it could have been.

Let us now look at the consequences of principle (4) that puts an upper limit to the quantitative value of happiness and suffering during any period.

We must begin by stating that even if one can plausibly maintain that there is an upper limit to the quantitative value of happiness during any period, it is very implausible to maintain that there is a limit to the negative quantitative value of suffering during any period. If an extra life that is not worth living is lived, this will always be bad. It might be rejoined that a reference to the value of quality would be sufficient to support this belief. But this is not the case: creating an extra life which only contains suffering will raise the level of the quality of life if all the already existing people's lives contain even more suffering than the extra life. Therefore if one maintains that suffering is always bad, suffering must always have quantitative value.

What we are going to look at is therefore the consequences of a development of principle (4) based on the following two beliefs: 1) there is an upper limit to the quantitative value of happiness during any period, and 2) there is no limit to the negative quantitative value of suffering.

Consider three worlds, all consisting of one billion people. In the first one, world (1), all lives are constantly of a high quality. The quality of these lives does not change, and they only consist of happiness and not of any suffering. In the second world, world (2), all lives are constantly of a much higher quality than the lives in world (1). However besides a lot of happiness they all consist of some suffering. In the third world, world (3), all lives but one are constantly of the same very high quality as the lives in world (2); thus all these lives but one consist only of happiness. However, one life in the billion is not worth living.

Let us imagine that the upper limit to the quantitative value of happiness and suffering has not been reached by any of these worlds.

If we compare world (1) with worlds (2) and (3), the latter two worlds will in one respect be better, because these will contain more happiness than world (1). In another respect worlds (2) and (3) will be worse, because they both consist of some suffering, which world (1) does not. We can plausibly believe that the positive quantitative value of the extra happiness in worlds (2) and (3) outweighs the negative quantitative value of suffering in these worlds. Worlds (2) and (3) will therefore be better than world (1). Let us then imagine that we enlarge worlds (2) and (3). This will have the following consequences: 1) The positive quantitative value of the extra happiness in worlds (2) and (3) will assymptotically approach its upper limit. 2) The negative quantitative value of the suffering in these worlds will increase beyond any limits. Thus, if we imagine the populations in worlds (2) and (3) to be large enough, these worlds will become worse than world (1) and ultimately even worse than no world at all. Even if one maintains that quality has value in the sense that it is bad if the level of the quality of life is lower than it could have been, the positive "qualitative" value of worlds (2) and (3) will be outweighed by their negative quantitative value, as the populations of the worlds are so vast.

These conclusions are of course totally unacceptable. We can avoid the conclusions concerning world (2) if we introduce Parfit's concept of compensated suffering: "Suffering is compensated if it comes within a life that is worth living. If it comes within a life that is not worth living, it is uncompensated." (*Reasons and Persons*, p. 408).

The value of these two different types of suffering Parfit explains as follows:

> It would always be bad if there is more uncompensated suffering. To this badness there is no upper limit. ... There are two ways in which there might be more compensated suffering: (1) There might be more suffering in a life now being lived that is worth living. (2) There might be an extra person who exists, with a life that is worth living, but containing some suffering. Of these two only (1) is bad. ... The suffering in these extra lives [(2)] has personal disvalue ... the personal disvalue of this extra suffering does not have moral disvalue. (*op. cit.*, p. 408 and 409).

I do not think this view on the value of compensated and uncompensated suffering is acceptable. First of all because I believe that suffering, compensated or not, must always be morally bad or in other words have moral disvalue. Secondly because Parfit's view leads to what I will call the Silly Conclusion: Imagine a population where the upper limit to the quantitative value of happiness and suffering has not been reached. Imagine also a choice between two possible extra lives – one which contains only happiness, and another which contains a little more happiness, but which apart from happiness also contains so much suffering that the life only barely is worth living. According to Parfit's view on the value of compensated and uncompensated suffering the morally relevant features in these lives narrow down to the amounts of happiness they contain. As there is more happiness in the second life this would be the better life to create.

Another view which would also enable us to avoid the conclusions concerning world (2) is the following: All suffering has always negative quantitative value. When happiness is used to outweigh compensated suffering there is no limit to the quantitative value of happiness during any period. Only when happiness is used to outweigh uncompensated suffering or a decrease in quality, is there an upper limit to the quantitative value of happiness during any period. In other words: When comparing different possible worlds, we first subtract for each world the total quantity of compensated suffering from the total quantity of happiness. It is the quantitative value of this amount of happiness and suffering – happiness minus compensated suffering – that has an upper limit.

Another possible way to explain the badness of the compensated suffering of Parfit's type (2) is to refer to the view that it is bad if the quality of life is lower than it could have been, and thus regard the alleged "non-badness" of this kind of suffering as "non-quantitative badness". Parfit actually opens up the possibility:

> It may be objected, "If this extra suffering is not bad, why would it have been better if these lives had not contained this suffering?" We could answer, "Because this would have made the quality of life even higher." (*op. cit.*, p. 408).

However by using this explanation we will still not avoid the following variant of the Silly Conclusion: Imagine a population where the upper limit to the quantitative value of happiness and suffering has not been reached. Imagine also a choice between two possible extra lives – one which contains only happiness, and another which contains a little more happiness, but which apart from the extra happiness also contains just enough extra suffering to outweigh the extra happiness. Thus the two lives are of the same quality. According to Parfit's view on the value of compensated and uncompensated suffering the morally relevant features in these lives narrow down to the amounts of happiness they contain and their overall quality. The lives are of the same quality but there is more happiness in the second life. Therefore this would be the better life to create.

As earlier mentioned, Parfit's concept of compensated and uncompensated suffering does not allow us to avoid the conclusion that world (3) can become worse than world (1) and even worse than no world at all. Moreover, if we accept this concept we are led to what Parfit calls

> the *Absurd Conclusion*: Consider the following two world histories: The first one, (A), is a world history in which for very many thousands of years there is constantly a population of one billion very happy people plus one man who does not have a life worth living. After these thousands of years the world ceases to exist. The second one, (B), is a world history where all the lives that are lived are identical with the lives in world history (A), in number as well as in quality. All these lives, however, exist at the same time, in one generation. According to the view under discussion, then although the lives in the two world histories are identical, both in number and in quality, world history (A) is very good, and world history (B) is very bad. World history (A) is very good because the quantitative value of the happiness and suffering in it never reaches its upper limit, and hence the positive quantitative value of happiness far outweighs the negative quantitative value of suffering. World history (B) is very bad because the quantitative value of the happiness and suffering in it has reached its upper limit, and hence the great negative quantitative value of suffering by far outweighs the positive quantitative value of happiness.

This conclusion arises unavoidably if one believes that 1) the positive quantitative value of happiness minus compensated suffering has, during any period, an upper limit, and 2) there is no limit to the negative quantitative value of uncompensated suffering, and stipulates 3) that compensated suffering is that which comes within lives that are worth living, and uncompensated suffering is that which comes within lives that are not worth living. Parfit believes that because of the absurdity of the conclusion we must reject the first belief. Another solution would be to change the stipulations about compensated and uncompensated suffering, stipulations which in my opinion are problematic. This I will return to later.

Another way to avoid the Absurd Conclusion is to omit the phrase "during any period" in belief (1). However, this will lead to a conclusion which is just as absurd: If one considers the value of every generation in world history (A) isolated, these are all very good; on the other hand world history (A) considered as a whole is very bad.

If we reject the view that there is a limit to the quantitative value of both suffering and happiness and still want to avoid both the Repugnant and the Absurd Conclusions, we must abandon the premise implied in the foregoing viz. that all levels of quality of life fit into a scale of moral value where the only "quality leap" takes place between levels of quality of life at which lives are not worth living, and levels of quality of life at which lives *are* worth living. We will say that this quality leap takes place at the Worth Living Level.

The Worth Living Level corresponds to zero on a cardinal scale. A consequence of this is that no number of lives whose quality is below or at the Worth Living Level can have as much positive value as any number of lives whose quality is above the Worth Living Level.

Parfit discusses two principles that involve more quality leaps, quality leaps with consequences similar to the above-mentioned. The first one is this:

(5) Quantity has value, i e.: Happiness and suffering have quantitative value. Quality has value – in the following way: Only happiness and suffering in lives whose quality is above or at a certain level (the Valueless Level), or below the Worth Living Level, have positive and negative quantitative value respectively.

The idea behind the Valueless Level is as follows: The Valueless Level is a level which is a little above the Worth Living Level. The happiness and suffering in lives whose quality is between these two levels have, of course, personal value for the people living these lives. However because of the low quality of the lives the happiness and suffering in them have no quantitative moral value. The second principle involving quality leaps that Parfit discusses actually covers two different principles. Parfit has not distinguished between these two principles, but the difference between them is quite important.

(6) Quantity has value, i e.: Happiness and suffering have quantitative value. Quality has value – in the following way: No amount of happiness minus suffering in lives whose quality is below a certain level (the Mediocre Level) and above, or at, the Worth Living Level can have as much moral value as any amount of happiness minus suffering in lives whose quality is above a certain higher level (the Blissful Level), *even if the amount of happiness minus suffering in the first mentioned lives has more personal value.*

(7) Quantity has value, i.e.: Happiness and suffering have quantitative value. Quality has moral value, because and only to the extent that it has *personal* value – in the following way: No amount of happiness minus suffering in lives whose quality is below a certain level (the Mediocre Level) and above, or at, the Worth Living Level can have as much moral value as any amount of happiness minus suffering in lives whose quality is above a certain higher level (the Blissful Level), *because no amount of happiness minus suffering in lives whose quality is below the Mediocre Level can have as much personal value as any amount of happiness minus suffering in lives whose quality is above the Blissful Level.*

Note that according to principle (7) we cannot always illustrate outcomes as we did in fig. 1!

Both principle (5), (6) and (7) can be extended to say that quality has value in the sense that it is bad if the level of the quality of life is lower than it could have been.

If principle (7) is not extended to say that quality has value in the sense that it is bad if the level of the quality of life is lower than it could have been, then according to this principle the moral value of an outcome coincides with the total personal value in the outcome. Thus it becomes clear that principle (7) is a variant of the Total Principle, a variant that makes some further empirical claims about the personal value of happiness minus suffering in lives at different levels of quality.

Unfortunately there are problems also with the three principles that include quality leaps. If we operate with the Valueless Level we are led to the following conclusions:

Repugnant "V": For any possible population, no matter how large it is or how high the quality of the life in it is, there must be some other possible population in which everybody has a life whose quality is at the Valueless Level, which, other things being equal, would be better if only this latter population is large enough.

Absurd "V": Consider a world in which 1) there is a vast population, 2) almost all the inhabitants have lives whose quality is just below the Valueless Level, and 3) one man in ten billion has a life not worth living. This world is worse than no world at all. The reason for this is the following: Happiness minus suffering in all the lives that are worth living has no quantitative value. The negative quantitative value of the lives that are not worth living will therefore be decisive for the value of the world. Even if one maintains that quality has value in the sense that it is bad if the level of the quality of life is lower than it could have been, the positive "qualitative" value of the world will be outweighed by its negative quantitative value, as the population of the world is so vast.

Conclusion "X": A population that consists of one person with a life whose quality is *at* the Valueless Level is better than one that consists of an extremely large number of people all with lives whose quality is *just below* this level.

Before we examine the consequences of operating with the Mediocre and the Blissful Levels, we must discuss the value of happiness minus suffering in lives whose quality is between or at these levels. Parfit has not pursued this discussion, but as we shall see, it is quite decisive.

The principle based on the Mediocre and the Blissful Levels is founded on the following suggestion: No amount of happiness minus suffering in lives whose quality is below a certain level can be as good as (have as moral value as) any amount of happiness minus suffering in lives whose quality is above a certain *higher* level. As I see it this suggestion is an attempt to avoid Conclusion "X" by inserting two levels instead of one. But unfortunately if this suggestion is to help us avoiding a conclusion very similar to Conclusion "X" it implies a selfcontradiction:

When operating with the Mediocre and the Blissful Levels there are two ways to evaluate the happiness minus suffering in lives whose quality is between or at one or other of the Mediocre and the Blissful Levels. 1) By adjusting amounts, happiness minus suffering in lives whose quality is below the Mediocre Level can be *as good as but not better than* happiness minus suffering in lives whose quality is between or at one or other of the Mediocre and the Blissful Levels, which in turn can be *as good as but not better than* happiness minus suffering in lives whose quality is above the Blissful Level. 2) By adjusting amounts, happiness minus suffering in lives whose quality is below the Mediocre Level can be *better than* happiness minus suffering in lives whose quality is between or at one or other of the Mediocre and the Blissful Levels, and happiness minus suffering in lives whose quality is between or at one or other of the Mediocre and the Blissful Levels can in turn be *better than* happiness minus suffering in lives whose quality is above the Blissful Level.

If we choose the first evaluation we are led to the following conclusion:

> *Conclusion "Y"*: A population that consists of one person with a life whose quality is *at* a certain level (the Mediocre Level or the level just higher than the Blissful Level) cannot be worse than one that consists of an extremely large number of people all with lives whose quality is *just below* this level.

If we want to avoid this conclusion we must choose the second evaluation. But by doing this it follows, because of the transitivity of the relation "better than", that happiness minus suffering in lives whose quality is below the Mediocre Level can be *better than* happiness minus suffering in lives whose quality is above the Blissful Level. But this clearly contradicts the suggestion we started out from.

The reason why the first evaluation does not lead to a self-contradiction is that "as good as" need not be a transitive relation. To illustrate this we can consider the three outcomes shown in fig. 3, which Parfit also discusses in *Reasons and Persons*.

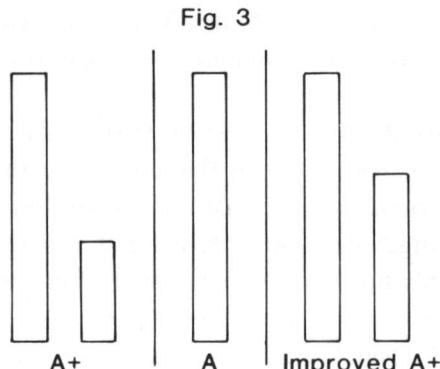

Fig. 3

A+   A   Improved A+

Again the width of the blocks shows the number of people living, the height shows how high the quality of these people's lives is.

I believe that the following beliefs are coherent: A+ is as good as A, A is as good as Improved A+, but A+ *is not as good as* Improved A+. The principles that could justify these beliefs are: Adding extra people to a set population does not increase moral value, but if extra people are to be added the quality of their lives should be as good as possible.

I am not sure Parfit would agree with this. Parfit believes that it is coherent to believe that A+ is not worse than A, that A is not worse than Improved A+ but that A+ *is worse than* Improved A+. Thus he believes that "not worse than" is not a transitive relation. But he states several times that the reason why the beliefs concerning A, A+ and Improved A are coherent is that "not worse than" does not imply "at least as good as". Thus apparently he believes that "at least as good as" *is* a transitive relation. As I believe that there is no relevant difference between "as good as" and "at least as good as" Parfit's view is in contradiction to mine. If one accepts Parfit's view then the first evaluation of the value of happiness minus suffering in lives whose quality is between or at one or other of the Mediocre and the Blissful Levels also leads to a contradiction.

If we choose the first evaluation we are led not only to Conclusion "Y" but also to the following conclusions:

> *Repugnant "MB" 1*: For any possible population, no matter how large it is or how high the quality of the life in it is, there must be some other possible population in which everybody has a life whose quality is at the

Mediocre Level, which, other things being equal, would be as good as the first, if only this latter population is large enough.

Repugnant "MB" 2: For any possible population consisting of lives whose quality is below or at the Blissfull Level, there must be some other possible population in which everybody has a life that is only barely worth living, which, other things being equal, would be as good as the first, if only this latter population is large enough.

Absurd "MB": Consider a world in which 1) there is a vast population, 2) almost all the inhabitants have lives whose quality is constantly just below the Mediocre Level, and 3) one man in ten billion has a life not worth living. This world is worse than no world at all. The reason for this is as follows: The negative quantitative value of happiness minus suffering in lives not worth living can outweigh the positive quantitative value of happiness minus suffering in lives whose quality is above the Blissful Level. Therefore the happiness minus suffering in the "mediocre" lives that cannot have as much positive quantitative value as any amount of happiness minus suffering in lives whose quality is above the Blissful Level, cannot have sufficient quantitative value to outweigh any amount of happiness minus suffering in the lives not worth living either. Hence the negative quantitative value of the lives not worth living will be decisive for the value of the world. Even if one maintains that quality has value in the sense that it is bad if the level of the quality of life is lower than it could have been, the positive "qualitative" value of the world will be outweighed by its negative quantitative value, as the population of the world is so vast.

Conclusion "Z": A population that consists of one person with a life whose quality is just above the Blissful Level is better than one that consists of an extremely large number of people all with lives whose quality is just below the Mediocre Level.

We can make some of the conclusions above more acceptable depending on where we fix the levels. Unfortunately, there are some opposite tendencies in this: Repugnant "V" becomes more acceptable, the higher we fix the Valueless Level, but if we do that, Absurd "V" becomes *less* acceptable – and vice versa.

Repugnant "MB" 1 becomes more acceptable, the higher we fix the Mediocre Level. But by raising the Mediocre Level Absurd "MB" becomes less acceptable and vice versa.

Repugnant "MB" 2 becomes more acceptable, the lower we fix the Blissful Level, Repugnant "MB" 1 becomes more acceptable, the higher we fix the Mediocre Level, but Conclusion "Z" becomes *less* acceptable the closer to each other we fix the Mediocre and the Blissful Levels.

Parfit believes that because of the above-mentioned conclusions, especially when they are connected as explained, we must abandon operating with these quality leaps. I.e. we must abandon the idea that there should be these quality leaps in the scale of either the moral or the personal value of the happiness minus suffering in a life. I agree with him on this.

III

What we have examined until now are what I believe to be the most decisive conclusions Parfit makes in Part 4 of *Reasons and Persons*. As we see Parfit has not found a solution to the Problem of Beneficence. I will now state an alternative to the principles discussed by Parfit which does not lead to any of the stated conclusions. Although I do not believe this alternative principle provides the right solution to the Problem of Beneficence, I will argue for the plausibility of some parts of the principle.

I mentioned earlier that I thought that Parfit's stipulation about compensated and uncompensated suffering was problematic. I will now explain why. We must remember that what we are discussing is the moral value of outcomes. We should therefore not start out by thinking about compensation as we normally do i.e. as personal compensation, but as moral compensation. Of course one can have the opinion that no suffering can be morally compensated for by happiness if this happiness does not arise in the same life as the suffering. This, however, is not my opinion. As a utilitarian I believe that suffering in one life can be morally compensated for by happiness in another life. In my opinion one should therefore stipulate that

A) suffering is compensated if it occurs within an outcome where people on an average have lives that are worth living, and

B) suffering is uncompensated if it occurs within an outcome where people on an average have lives that are not worth living.

With these stipulations we can formulate a variant of principle (4) that estimates the relative values of quantity and quality, and that does not lead to either the Repugnant or the Absurd Conclusion.

A consequence of using these stipulations is that all happiness and all suffering count equally much in the estimation of the value of an outcome. Therefore, we can omit the two concepts "happiness" and "suffering" if we use the concept "net-happiness" (happiness minus suffering) when formulating the principle.

(8) Quantity has value – in the following way: Net-happiness has quantitative value, but: The quantitative value of net-happiness during any period has an upper limit. As the actual quantity of net-happiness increases, the quantitative value of extra net-happiness declines and asymptotically approaches zero.
Quality has value – in the following way: When the Level of the quality of life is higher, there is a higher upper limit to the quantitative value of net-happiness during any period.

The reason why principle (8) avoids the Absurd Conclusion is that it gives suffering and happiness equal value. Therefore, suffering can always be outweighed by happiness, if the positive personal value of happiness is just as great or greater than the negative value of suffering.

The reason why principle (8) avoids the Repugnant Conclusion is of course that it sets an upper level to the quantitative value of net-happiness, and that this level is higher when the level of the quality of life is higher.

Why does this principle not provide the right solution to the Problem of Beneficence? The decisive suggestion in principle (8) is that the quantitative value of happiness and suffering during any period has an upper limit, a limit that becomes higher when the level of the quality of life is higher. This suggestion cannot be derived from the two values of quantity and quality. It is not only quality that limits the quantitative value of happiness during any period. According to this solution the quantitative value of extra happiness in extra lives depends on 1) the level of the quality of life, and 2) the number of people that already exist. But I do not see why happiness in person number fifty billion should be morally worth less than happiness in person number two. This is because the number of people that already exist in my opinion is not a morally relevant boundary.

Furthermore principle (8) leads to a conclusion similar to the Absurd Conclusion: A certain very large population would have less value if it were to exist in one generation than it would have if it were spread out over time. The reason for this is, of course, that the upper limit to the quantitative value of happiness and suffering is set only for quantities *during any period*. Thus if we spread a population out over time we can make sure that the upper limit to the quantitative value of happiness and suffering never reaches its upper limit.

This conclusion can be avoided if the time dependence in the limitation of the quantitative value of happiness and suffering is omitted. By doing this the value of extra happiness in extra lives depends on the number of people that have existed or already exist. In my opinion this is also unacceptable. The number of people that have existed or already exist cannot be a morally relevant boundary either.

"VALUE" IN TURN-OF-THE-CENTURY PHILOSOPHY AND SOCIOLOGY

MOGENS BLEGVAD

The Royal Danish Academy of Sciences and Letters

I

The period around the turn of the century has recently become a focus of interest in many branches of historical research. It is, indeed, a very interesting period, marked by rapid and profound changes in practically all areas of society and culture, and by violent tensions between the old and the new, some of which tensions were released in the Great War of 1914-1918 and the revolutions which it brought about. The war was widely viewed as the end of, or at least the beginning of the end of, civilization,[1] and it is natural to take its conclusion, which should not be dated earlier than 1920 when the last peace treaties were signed, as marking the end of the period in question.

It is more difficult to indicate its beginning; historical periods are ususally not sharply demarcated, and where it is reasonable to put the dividing line depends on the purpose to be served by the periodization and the point of view adopted in the particular investigation. Within the field of intellectual history various points in time in the interval between 1870 and 1890 offer themselves as candidates. For the purpose of the present study which concentrates on the prominence given to the concept of value by philosophers and by the pioneers of the new science of sociology, the period should be considered as beginning rather early in the interval indicated. The attempts by philosophers to develop a general theory of value and the contemporaneous emergence of sociology as an independent field of study are, as I shall try to show, not unrelated. They are at least connected by having a common root in the developments in the field of economics which started in the 1870ies.

Among the intellectual innovations that characterize the turn-of-the-century period some of the most conspicuous belong to physics. The discovery of X-rays, radioactivity and the energy quantum, the introduction of the relativity theories and the creation of the Rutherford-Bohr atomic model changed the picture of the physical world radically. The age-old programme of reducing all physical phenomena to mechanics had finally to be given up for ever, and the world of electrons, atoms, quanta, etc. looked much more different from our ordinary everyday world than that of the older physical theories.

Other sciences, too, underwent important changes, and in literature, the arts and music new movements arose which signified a definite break with the past. "Modernism" has, at least in literature, been the label used to cover the breaking-up of the old norms that happened in these cultural fields.[2] A general trend which found its expression in many fields, most explicitly in philosophy, was a change in the conception of man. The active, conative, and emotive aspects of the mind received increasing attention, and even cognition was no longer conceived as a passive reception of information about reality or as the result of a God-given pure reason. Knowing is an activity, and man is not only a knower, but also, and primarily, an actor and appraisor, driven by impulses that are not alway fully conscious – let alone rational. Nietzsche was the inspiring pioneer for this new point of view, but it was developed further in thinkers like Bergson, William James and Freud .

These developments, however, differed among themselves. In some cases the emphasis was put on the irrational and unconscious sources of behaviour, in others human activity was modelled on the concept of rational choice between means to given purposes. The latter approach necessarily put human values as guides for such choices into focus, but also Nietzsche made values central in demanding an "Umwertung aller Werte". It is therefore natural that the idea of a general theory of value emerged just in this period. But "value" is used in many senses. Some of these square well with a conception of man as a rational chooser while others are employed to express moral and social constraints on such choices, constraints which may be connected with less rational motivational sources. Hence, the idea of a general theory of value is not unproblematic, and those who tried to develop such a theory ran into great difficulties. The same goes for the sociological pioneers who assigned a major role to values in their theories of social action as well as in their conceptions of how social phenomena may be investigated scientifically.

II

The first two philosophical works having what in English would be "theory of value" in their title appeared in the 1890ies. They were written by two Austrian philosophers, Alexius Meinong and Christian von Ehrenfels, and Vienna, where they both got their education, was one of the most important scenes of the struggle between the new and the old around the turn of the century.[3] During the reign of Emperor Franz Joseph the Austrian Empire was fraught with contradictions and paradoxes – a multitude of nationalities held together by the person of the emperor, who, however, as the result of defeat in foreign policy and war (1859, 1866) had to accept a partition between Austria and Hungary and a constitution, which gave the "Bürgerthum" part in the political power; great splendour at the court and among the wealthy as against poverty among the industrial proletariat and backwardness in the rural areas; a conservatism impersonated in the emperor who was against all kinds of change, as against a radicalism which, since it could not find a political outlet, expressed itself in daring innovations in art, literature, and music.

From earlier periods two opposed sets of values had been inherited, the one centered on Enlightenment ideas of reason and progress, the other based on Counterreformation Catholicism. The second gave rise to a kind of aestheticism, while the first became the basis of a bourgeois liberalism, which stressed freedom, not the least in economic matters, within strict rules of morals and law. The centre of this liberalism was the salons of leading business families, often of Jewish origin, and the law faculty of the university. This faculty, together with the faculty of medicine, was among the most respected in Europe. They had been created by empress Maria Theresia and joined to the theological and philosophical faculties of the old, Jesuit dominated university. The law professors and their colleagues in medicine were standard-bearers of the enlightenment idea of scientific knowledge as the source of progress, but among their students an opposition against this attitude gradually emerged; it embraced nationalism – in the form of pan-germanism among the German speaking non-jewish majority – and socialism, or at least sympathy with the working class. It critizised corruption and inefficiency in government.

Schopenhauer, Nietzsche and Wagner were the heroes of an influential group of students who in 1871 formed a "Leseverein der deutschen Studenten Wiens".[4] This organization arranged pilgrimages to Bayreuth, and some of its leaders wrote an enthusiastic "fan-letter" to Nietzsche in 1879.[5] Gustav Mahler, among others, was influenced by this movement, which, to use a Nietzschean term, stood for a more or less Dionysean attitude. At a meeting of the "Leseverein" the philosopher Franz Brentano in 1876 warned against this attitude and defended the ideal of objective scholarship. In view of the role Brentano played in the development of Austrian theory of value – he was not only the teacher of Meinong and v. Ehrenfels, but worked through his life on developing his own philosophy of value – this is noteworthy.

A later instance of a Viennese philosophy professor attacking an expression of a Dionysean attitude was the uproar around Gustav Klimt's paintings for the main hall of the new university building on the Ringstrasse. After having in 1894 been asked to paint allegorical presentations of three of the faculties, Klimt founded the oppositional Secession movement and changed his style, and when in 1900 and the following years he exhibited first "Philosophy" and then "Medicine" and "Law", the professors objected vigorously. In their opinion the paintings in their style and symbolism expressed an anti-rationalism quite incongruent with the purpose.[6] Their main spokesman was Friedrich Jodl, since 1896 professor of philosophy. Jodl was born and educated in Munich where he got his doctor's degree on a dissertation on Hume. He went to Prague in 1885, and from there to Vienna. Apart from Hume it was Feuerbach, Mill, and Comte who had influenced him. His main work is the two-volume *Geschichte der Ethik* (1882-89) and his position was a kind of utilitarianism.[7] That a man of such convictions should feel called upon to collect protests from 87 collegues against Klimt's "Philosophy" is understandable. "Law" which expresses more sympathy with the criminal than admiration for 'veritas', 'justitia' and 'lex' did not please the professors in that faculty. Among these were one of the most admired teachers, the economist Carl Menger.

Menger is the founder of the Austrian maginalist school in economic theory and there is much evidence for the importance of the teachings of this school for the attempts by Austrian philosophers to develop a general theory of value.[8] The conditions at the University of Vienna were at that time favourable for influences across the faculty boundaries, and the lectures of both Menger and Brentano were popular with students from outside their special fields. Alexius Meinong e.g. followed Menger's course in economic theory the first year he taught it as a professor (1872-73).[9]

III

In order to understand how the introduction of the marginalist point of view in economics could inspire philosophers in this direction it is necessary to take a brief look at the development of economic value theory. We need not, however, go further back in time than to Adam Smith. When he undertook to account for "the nature and causes of the wealth of nations" he took it for granted that it is necessary, in order to explain price formation and the ensuing remuneration of the various factors of production and their owners, to assume that the products of economic activity – goods and services – have value. But he pointed out that one must distinguish between what he called "value in use" and "value in exchange".[10] In order that something may have economic importance, enter into economic transactions, it must be of some use, it must somehow be able to contribute to the satisfaction of human needs and wishes. How much one can get in exchange for it, or how high a price it can command in a money economy, is another matter. One might expect its value in exchange to be determined by its usefulness, but here another factor enters, one which Smith's teacher Francis Hutcheson, following an old tradition, called "scarcity". Smith gives a famous example: "The things which have the greatest value in use have frequently little or no value in exchange; and, on the contrary, those which have the greatest value in exchange have frequently little or no value in use. Nothing is more useful than water; but it will purchase scarce anything; scarce anything can be had in exchange for it. A diamond, on the contrary, has scarce any value in use; but a very great quantity of other goods may frequently be had in exchange for it".[11]

In the short run the values in exchange, the relative prices, are determined by supply and demand, but in the long run they will approach what Smith calls "the natural prices". What are they? Here we must remember that his main purpose was to show that the mercantilist policies did not further but, on the contrary, impeded the growth of a nation's wealth. He ascribed to the mercantilist economists the false conception of such wealth as consisting in the stock of precious metals (= money) owned by the nation in question. Actually it consists in the amount of goods and services available to the population in a certain period of time. But these are of different kinds, and since both the absolute and the relative prices fluctuate we cannot compare a nations's wealth in one period with that in another by comparing the sums of the products of the quantities of the various goods available with their unit prices. Smith approaches this problem by pointing out that the production of goods requires that people work, and therefore suggests that the value of a collection of goods should be measured by the amount of labour ("toil and trouble") one can avoid by using it to buy ("command") labour from others. The natural (relative) price of a good is accordingly determined by this amount.[12]

Smith might also have said that it is determined by the amount of labour required to produce it (the socalled 'embodied labour'), and in some places he actually seems to have said so. But, as he emphasizes, the production of a certain amount of corn requires not only labour, but also land and capital, e.g. to pay the wages until the corn is harvested and sold. And those who own the land and provide the capital must also be remunerated out of the money which the sale brings in. Recent scholarship, which has profited by the publication of Smith's *Lectures in Jurisprudence*, has shown that he did not confuse "demanded labour" and "embodied labour", as David Ricardo accused him of doing, but consistently regarded the former as the measure of value.[13]

Ricardo, on the contrary, based his theory of value on embodied labour, which, by the way, obliged him to make some rather artificial assumptions to explain why rent and profit do not influence relative prices. Malthus, on the other hand, stuck to commanded labour, and kept up a running debate with Ricardo on this question. The last contribution to this debate is a letter written by Ricardo not long before his death, in which he concludes that neither Malthus nor he himself had succeded in finding a fixed measure of value.[14] In the further development of classical economics Ricardo's embodied labour theory of value prevailed. Even John Stuart Mill whose *Principles of Political Economy* appeared 31 years after the similarly named main work by Ricardo, builds on this theory, although as an utilitarian and a follower of Bentham he could be expected to emphasize "value in use". Bentham, as a matter of fact, was among the few in this period who did so. He not only claimed that it is the prospect of obtaining pleasure or evading pain which motivates us (psychological hedonism), but also declared pleasure to be the only thing which in itself has positive value, and pain to be the only thing which in itself has negative value (axiological hedonism). Economic goods have value in so far as their consumption can produce pleasure or reduce pain.

Note that in these last sentences we have encountered two distinctions of importance whenever we speak of values. In the last sentence "value" is used in such a way that to say that something has value means that it is good, while "value" in the next to last sentence is used as a variable rangeing from positive to negative. The first use is dominant in common language while the latter is preferable in theoretical work. The second distinction is that between having value in itself and having value as a means.[15]

IV

Bentham maintained that the pleasure or satisfaction which can derived from a certain amount of a good which one has acquired diminishes with the amount of the said good one already commands. This is called the law of diminishing utility. By formulating this law Bentham became one of the precursors of the marginalist revolution in economic theory. Another precursor was the German Hermann Heinrich Gossen who in his main work which appeared in 1854 warned against conceiving value as something objective and relative adhering to goods as the labour theory of value does. Instead we must take value as dependent on human thoughts, feelings, and desires, which vary in a number of directions, and consequently as something subjective and relative. Gossen also put forward the law of diminishing utility (which Walras later named Gossen's first law) independently of Bentham. He made a further important step by formulating his "second law": when a person consumes goods of different kinds he will tend to distribute the money available to him on the various goods such that the pleasure he gets from the last unit of money spent on each is the same for all goods. This means that he can gain nothing by distributing his expenditures differently.[16]

This pattern of thought and these "laws" formed the basis of the theories developed by Menger, and by William Jevons and Léon Walras who at the same time, but independently of him, founded marginalist economics.[17] There are important differences between their theories, but they all agree that "a thing is not a good because other goods have been employed in its production. On the contrary, it is clear that one employs goods to produce something because this is a good", as Menger puts it.[18] That value should be considered to be subjective is clear from Menger's definition: "Value is not something adhering to goods, no quality belonging to them, but the importance that concrete goods have for economically active men because they are aware that the satisfaction of their needs depends on their command of the goods in question".[19]

Jevons quotes Adam Smith on water and diamonds, and comments as follows: "It is sufficiently plain that, when Smith speaks of water as being highly useful and yet devoid of purchasing power, he means water in abundance, that is to say, water so abundantly supplied that it has exerted its full useful effect, or its total utility. Water, when it becomes very scarce ... acquires exeedingly great purchasing power ...".[20] One must therefore distinguish between "value in use" = "total utility", purchasing power = ratio of exchange, and finally marginal value, which Jevons here calls "final degree of utility" and defines as "the degree of utility of the last addition, or the next possible addition of a very small, or indefinitely small, quantity of the existing stock". It decreases as the existing stock increases (Gossen's first law), and it is it which we have to look for in order to explain the price.[21]

By dissolving the water-diamond paradox in this way the marginalists were able to do justice to the common sense conviction that economic value must, after all, be a question of usefulness, of ability to contribute – directly or indirectly – to the satisfaction of human wants and desires. This further opened the possibility of treating economic value and other kinds of value similarly. This had not been possible on the basis of the labour theory of value. According to the latter, economic value is an objective property, and values of other kinds which are not related to an amount of labour, such as artistic value, cannot be brought in line with economic value. But it seems not unreasonable to say e.g. that artistic value has to do with the degree of aesthetic pleasure the object may give rise to. In this manner artistic value becomes subjective like utility value, and perhaps all kinds of value may be subsumed under a general concept of value defined in terms of subjective phenomena such as satisfaction, pleasure, desire, or the like. And perhaps the marginalist theory might be generalized into a general theory of value.

V

The philosopher who most emphatically embraced this idea was Christian von Ehrenfels. As mentioned in section II, he had been educated in Vienna, where he entered the university in 1879 as a student of law.[22] He soon gave up law for philosophy, where his main teachers were Franz Brentano (1838-1917) and Alexius Meinong (1853-1920). When the latter moved to Graz von Ehrenfels followed him and graduated there in 1885. Three years later he habilitated in Vienna with a dissertation on feeling and will. Two years later appeared an essay (*Über Gestaltqualitäten* (On Gestalt Qualities)) in which he introduced an idea which was later developed by the important school of Gestalt psychology. When in 1896 Friedrich Jodl left Prague for Vienna he succeeded him as professor of philosophy, and in 1897-98 he published his main work, *System der Werttheorie I -II*. In addition to philosophical works he later wrote unorthodox publications on eugenics and sexual morality, propagating for "racial hygiene" and polygamy. He tried to show that his opinions on these points followed from his theory of value. He retired in 1929, at the age of 70, and died in 1932.

Chr. v. Ehrenfels had broad cultural interests, e.g. in poetry – he wrote a number of dramas – and music, which he studied with Anton Bruckner, while Richard Wagner was his hero. Among his friends and acquaintancies were Freud, Masaryk, Kafka, and his neighbour in Prague, the economist Friedrich von Wieser (1851-1926).[23] Von Wieser was one of Carl Menger's main pupils, together with his brother-in-law Eugen Böhm-Bawerk (1951-1914). It has become customary to label Menger and his pupils the first Austrian school of value theory. The second consists then of Brentano, Meinong and von Ehrenfels.[24] Although there were close connections between the economists and the philosophers – I have mentioned a couple of instances of this – and although there is no doubt that the latter were inspired by the development in economic theory made by Menger and his pupils,[25] it is misleading by this labelling to conceal the fundamental difference between the two "schools". Menger and his pupils were economists, occupied with the problems of their discipline, primarily with the analysis of microeconomic relationships, although both Böhm-Bawerk and von Wieser by serving for periods as minsters of finance showed willingness to use their theoretical insight in practical politics. The philosophers, on the other hand, aspired to create theories of value covering a wider field, including ethics and aesthetics. Their starting point was the "descriptive psychology" which Brantano had expounded in his *Psychologie vom empirischen Standpunkt* from 1874. Since also the Austrian economists based their theory of value on presuppositions concerning the working of the human mind (e.g. Gossen's first law), it could be said that the two schools had in common the use of a psychological approach. Brentano's psychology was, however, of a special character. It is not empirical in the ordinary sense, only in the sense that it is founded on our immediate experience of what it means to perceive, feel, or will something. Its main task is to classify the mental phenomena and to formulate laws for their intuitively given "natural affinities". This, by the way, is the root of Husserl's "Wesenschau" – Husserl was among those Viennese students who were "seduced" by Brentano into leaving their original field, in his case mathematics, for philosophy – as well as of the aprioristic method of Austrian economics.[26]

Brentano maintained that intentionality is the essence of mental phenomena; they are all directed towards something, a perception is a perception of something, an emotion also has an object, etc. He criticized the identification of content and object of consciousness which other psychologists had adopted from the British empiricists. He also rejected the tripartition of mental phenomena introduced by Tetens and Kant. Instead of distinguishing between cognition, emotion, and will, he introduced another tripartition: "Vorstellung" (idea), "Urteil" (judgment),[27] "Liebe und Hass" (love and hate). The last mentioned category includes emotions, desires, attitudes, decisions, etc. Meinong and von Ehrenfels wanted here to distinguish between emotions or feelings on the one hand, and desires on the other, but disagreed on which of these types of phenomena constitutes evaluations. According to Meinong it is the first, while von Ehrenfels defined value in terms of desire. We attribute value to things, because we desire them. But, as Meinong had pointed out, there are things which we attibute value to without desiring them, simply because we have them already. So a more satisfactory formulation is the following: "We ascribe value to those things which we in fact desire, or which we would desire if we were not convinced of their existence. The value of a thing is its desirability ... The stronger we desire or would desire an object, the higher value does that object possess for us".[28] What we really desire is accordingly either the existence of something or the possession of it. "In the latter case the desire also relates to an existence, not of the thing itself, but of our power of disposing over it, and at the same time it is directed to a non-existence: the absence of all disturbances which would inhibit this power...".[29]

What is then this value actually? It cannot be a property of the object. If we think so, we are mislead by the language we use.[30] The correct answer is the following: "Value is a relation between an object and a subject, which expresses that the subject either in fact desires the object, or would desire it if it were not convinced of its existence".[31] So "value" is something relational and subjective.

VI

It is useful to compare this conception of value with those of Bentham and Carl Menger. For Bentham what has value (in itself) is something subjective, namely pleasure or pain, but his value concept is not relational or relative. Pleasure is something good, and pain something bad, irrespective of who has it, I, Mrs. Hansen, or a dog. To Bentham values are absolute. I suspect that they are so for Menger too. Because of the vagueness of the expression "importance" in his definition, the question is difficult to decide, but the most natural interpretation is that economic value for him is instrumental value. That which has value in itself is the satisfaction an economic good can give, directly in the case of consumer goods, which he calls goods of the first order, indirectly in the case of goods of higher order, which are used to produce goods of an order one step lower than their own. He and his pupils were mostly concerned with the socalled problem of imputation. The value of goods of a higher order is dependent on the value of those goods of a lower order which they serve to produce,[32] but the fact that goods may have alternative uses, may be substituted for another, and may be complementary, makes it a problem to determine how much value a good of a higher order receives in this way.

Value can then be defined in terms of desires and their satisfaction in two different ways, which should not be confused. One is to say with Bentham (and Menger) that the satisfaction has absolute value, the other is to say with von Ehrenfels that desires confer value on their objects. One important difference is that according to the first kind of definitions value is something of which there ought to be as much as possible, while this does not follow in the second case, since one way of creating more value would here be to create more desire, which can be done by frustrating the person in question.[33] Another important difference is the following: according to the second conception value is a relational notion, which means that we always have to ask: "value for whom?" and that it is without meaning to add values for different subjects, while according to the first conception, value is an absolute notion, and if it is possible to measure the pleasure or satifaction of different subjects on the same scale, it makes sense to speak of sums of values, even thought the pleasures or satisfactions which have the individual values belong to different subjects.[34] This of course is what utilitarians do.

VII

Although British by origin utilitarianism had some adherents in the German world around the turn of the century. Friedrich Jodl has already been mentioned (in section II), and before him Georg von Gizycki (professor in Berlin 1851-95) had written on Hume and expounded an ethics based on the greatest happiness principle. Also von Ehrenfels had undoubtedly inclinations in this direction, but since he wants to account for ethical values as subsumable under his general concept of value, it is questionable whether it really is possible for him to develop a normative ethics of a utilitarian stamp, when the relativist character of this concept and the distinction emphasized in the previous section is taken into consideration. In fact he often tends to shy away from normative, prescriptive pronouncements, and to limit himself to decribing moral phenomena. Still, merely his use of the term "das Wohl der Gesamtheit" (the general weal) seems to put him in the utilitarian camp. Another problem: his general theory of value is obviously meant as a generalization of the economic theory of Menger and his pupils, but Menger's concept of value is, also according to von Ehrenfels, of another kind than his own, i.e. of the absolutist kind.

On this latter problem his first publications on value theory, a series of papers entitled *Werttheorie und Ethik* (Theory of value and ethics) from 1893-94, throw some light.[35] In these he blames Fr. v. Wieser, who is his main source for economic value theory, for not having defined "value", and Menger for having used the vague term "Bedeutung" in his definition.[36] But his main complaints are that the economists limit their value concept in two directions, and that it rests on an untenable presupposition. One limitation consists in their taking concrete goods to be what is valued. They are not aware that what they really mean is that the ownership of the goods has value, and that this is a special case of value being attributed to the existence of something (see section V).[37]

The second limitation consists in the economists only dealing with instrumental values ("Wirkungswerte"), not with intrinsic values ("Eigenwerte").[38] When Menger distinguishes between goods of first order and goods of higher order, he does not consider the first to have intrinsic value; all economic values are instrumental, the intrisic value of the "Bedürfnisbefriedigung" (satisfaction of needs) which they can give – directly in the case of goods of first order, indirectly in the case of the others – being presupposed.[39]

Von Ehrenfels cannot, however, follow Menger in considering the satisfaction of needs as having intrinsic value. This would presuppose that satisfaction is the only thing we can desire, which is not the case. "Glücksförderung" (the promotion of happiness) is in fact not the only thing we desire.[40] Only by recognizing this and by removing the limitations is it possible to establish a general theory of value.

How can an account of ethical values be fitted into such a theory founded on a value concept defined in terms of desire?

Von Ehrenfels deals with this in the second volume of his main work.[41] Ethical values are those attributed to actions, motives, and persons in acts of moral approval and disapproval. Further analysis shows that the primary objects of moral evaluation are the presence or absence of "Gefühls- und Begehrsdispositionen" (tendencies to feel and desire), and that the most important of these in our culture is "allgemeine Menschenliebe" (benevolence).[42] In other cultures it may be different – at some points von Ehrenfels approaches a moral relativism.

The tendencies which are approved, respectively disapproved morally seem in general to share the character of "Gemeinnützlichkeit" (general usefulness), respectively "Gemeinschädlichkeit" (general harmfulness). "One might therefore be tempted to follow the widespread utilitarian ethics in taking general usefulness and harmfulness to be the directly determining factor in ethical valuation".[43] Various considerations, again mostly of a descriptive-psychological nature, force one however to modify this utilitarian view considerably, "although the basic tendency may be preserved".[44]

Von Ehrenfels discusses whether ethical value should be considered as "Wirkungswert" (instrumental value) in accordance with the utilitarian view, or as "Eigenwert" (intrinsic value). He states that those who attribute intrinsic value to "das Wohl der Gesamtheit" (the common weal) and are aware that a morally approved tendency furthers this will consider this tendency to have instrumental value. But often ethical values are experienced as intrinsic, because moral approval or disapproval does not presuppose any conscious consideration of causal relationships.[45] Again psychological observations are called upon to decide ethical questions.

What is "das Wohl der Gesamtheit"? Von Ehrenfels admits that this is a very ambiguous term, but his prolonged and complicated discussion results nevertheless in a statement to the effect that perhaps all its many senses cover the same reality.[46] So again we approach a utilitarian position, but I have not found any place where von Ehrenfels identifies the common weal with a sum of values, which of course would have been in more explicit conflict with his relativistic concept of value. Through his whole discussion of ethics he seems to try to balance between giving a descriptive-psychological account of moral evaluation and developing a normative ethics of a utilitarian stamp from which in his later works he could draw practical conclusions. He is eager to emphasize the special character and importance of ethical values but nevertheless defends "the application of the general principles of the theory of value to the phenomena of ethical action, feeling, and judging".[47]

VIII

Also von Ehrenfels' teacher Alexius Meinong wanted to include ethical values in a general theory of value developed on the basis of psychological observations. As mentioned above (section V) he disagreed with von Ehrenfels on the question whether it is desires or emotions (feelings) which constitute value experience. In his first publication in this field, *Psychologisch-ethische Untersuchungen zur Werth-theorie* from 1894, he presented a theory in which emotions as mental acts have values as their objects. It is, however, not the emotion as such which constitutes a value, but the ability of something to produce the emotion.[48] Meinong accepts that this implies that values are relative to the valuing subject.[49]

However, he could not in the long run accept that this is the case with ethical values; there is, after all, a significant difference between the kind of goodness we find in a good man and his conduct, and that which we experience when we eat our favourite dish.[50] When towards the end of his life, he prepared a second edition of *Untersuchungen* he therefore not only changed its title (to *Zur Grundlegung der allgemeinen Werttheorie*), but also modified his theory radically.[51] In the meantime he had developed his socalled "Gegenstandstheorie" and a concept of emotional presentation which allowed him to make such radical changes. He characterized his former theory as psychologistic and maintained the existence of what he called "Nicht-persönliche Werte" (non-personal values). Inspired by Brentano he worked with an analogy between cognition and emotion. In the treatise on emotional presentations he writes e.g.: "I say of the sky at one time that it is blue, and at another that it is beautiful, and the sky appears to be no less ascribed a property in the latter case than in the former, the one property being just as well conveyed by a feeling as the other by an idea, so we could not do better than ascribe the function of presentation, which everyone ascribes to ideas, to feelings".[52] Just as the intended objects of perceptions and ideas must be distinguished from their contents – according to the Brentanian philosophy – the property of something which a feeling presents to us must be distinguished from the quality of the feeling. In order for such a presentation to be an evaluation the feeling has to be linked to a judgment. Judgments, as all mental phenomena, have objects. Meinong calls them "objectives". What is evaluated is therefore always a possible state af affairs. This is not very different from von Ehrenfels' point of view.

The quotation from the treatise on emotional presentation shows that for Meinong not only ethical, but also aesthetic valuations belong to the non-personal kind which we require others to share, in contradistinction to the personal ones where we are willing to accept that "tastes differ". The introduction of this distinction constitutes the major change in Meinong's theory of value. But how can we know whether an experienced value is personal or non-personal? We need an objective test, apart from our willingness or unwillingness to accept disagreements.

The test cannot be whether people agree or not; in the case of a non-personal value I can have the right evaluation, despite the fact that all others disagree, and in the case of a personal one it may so happen that we all share the same taste.

Are non-personal and personal values really species of the same genus? This is denied, with good reasons, in a somewhat neglected Swedish dissertation from 1937 *Über die Möglichkeit einer Werteinteilung* by the late Sven Edvard Rodhe.[53] When in a paper from 1912 Meinong gives the following definition: "The value of an object consists in the fact that a subject takes interest in it, might take interest in it, or should reasonably take interest in it",[54] one should notice that only of non-personal values can it ever be said that one should "take interest in" them.[55] Further, Meinong seems to introduce potentiality (might take interest in) in order to mitigate the contrast between the factual "take interest in" and the normative "should take interest in". This does not really help; we still have two quite different concepts: subjective value which is established merely by being experienced, and objective value which can be correctly or incorrectly experienced or judged. And we have not been told how to distinguish the two.

IX

Brentano, in addition to inspiring Meinong and von Ehrenfels to develop general theories of value on the basis of his descriptive psychology, himself worked through the years with the value problems.[56] He lectured at the University of Vienna on "practical philosophy", but only many years after his death were these lectures published under the title *Grundlegung und Aufbau der Ethik*.[57] Until then his theory had mostly been known from a lecture *Vom Ursprung sittlicher Erkenntnis* which he published in 1889.[58]

In this lecture Brentano refers to the tripartition of mental acts into "Vorstellen", "Urteilen" and "Gemütsbewegungen" which he also calls "Liebe und Hass". It is these last mentioned which constitute the world of values. That is good in itself (has positive intrinsic value) which it is correct to love for its own sake – "love" being taken in a very wide sense (see section V). The bad-in-itself is that which it is correct to hate for its own sake. That something (A) is better than something else (B) means that it is correct to prefer A to B. Values are not measurable, more or less value is not a question of stronger or less strong love.[59] Only mental phenomena have intrinsic value, but many other kinds of things have instrumental value (Brentano uses the terms "primary" and "secondary" goods).[60] Economic goods have only instrumental value.

Although values are not measurable according to Brentano,[61] he nevertheless formulates a "principle of the summation of good": "To further the good throughout this great whole (every living thing upon the earth, present and future) as far as possible – this is clearly the correct end in life, and all our actions should be centered around it. It is the supreme imperative upon which all others depend".[62] It is very doubtful whether this principle is implied by, or even compatible with, Brantano's account of value.

A crucial point in his theory is of course his answer to the question how correct love or hate differs from incorrect. The answer is founded on an analogy between cognition and evaluation. Judgments may be evident ("einsichtige") or blind (not evident). A judgment is correct or true if it is either evident or, if blind, agrees with (has the same quality and the same subject as) an evident judgment.[63] Brentano rejects the correspondence theory of truth.[64] Now "Gemütsbewegungen" may have a property analogous to evidence, and so also one analogous to truth. In some remarks on love and hate, which he dictated in 1907, he stated: "there is, in the sphere of the emotions ("auf dem Gebiet des Gemüts") a correct loving and hating and an incorrect loving and hating. This may seem to be the analogue of correct acceptance or affirmation and correct rejection or denial, but it is essentially different".[65] If the analogue were complete a "law of excluded middle" should be valid in the "sphere of emotions" as, according to Brentano it is in the sphere of judgments. And in the lecture of 1889 he actually formulated such a law: "Of the two opposing attitudes, love and hate, being pleased and being displeased, in every instance one of them is correct and the other incorrect".[66] But he later gave it up, according to Oskar Kraus because he saw that there may be axiologically indifferent things.[67]

Now, Brentano of course meant that there are "blind" emotions like there are blind judgments, although he uses other terms, and one might think that the objects of such emotions have what Meinong called personal value. But just as a blind judgment may be correct – namely if it agrees with an evident judgment – so a blind love may be correct under the analogous condition. And the object of a correct love has non-personal (objective) value. So the distinction between the kind of valuation where we are prepared to say "de gustibus non est disputandum", and those where we are not, cannot be explicated on the basis of Brentano's distinction between the blind and the evident. One might perhaps say that something which only has personal value is such that no love or hate of it can be evident, and that accordingly there is in such cases no question of correctness, but we have not been presented with any objective criterion for distinguishing these cases. Quite apart from the difficulties any intuitionist theory encounters, Brentano's theory of value does not succeed in covering all kinds of value.[68]

In my opinion none of the members of "the second Austrian school" has succeeded in creating a theory of value in which economic value and ethical value have been subsumed under a general concept and at the same time been distinguished correctly. The idea of generalizing the economic theory of value of "the first school" seems not to have been very fruitful. The philosophers have escaped some of the errors which a hedonist utilitarianism involves, but what they have put in its stead is not much better.

X

In the year 1887 when von Ehrenfels published the first volume of *System der Werttheorie*, a quite different book which was destined to become a classic in the new science of sociology appeared: Ferdinand Tönnies' *Gemeinschaft und Gesellschaft*. Also in 1887 Émile Durkheim in Bordeaux started his first series of lectures in social science on "solidarité sociale" (social solidarity) in which he set out the argument of what was to become another classic, *De la division du travail social* (The Division of Labour) of 1893. In 1890 Georg Simmel, a Privatdozent at the university of Berlin, published his first sociological work *Über sociale Differenzierung*. The fourth of the generation which established sociology as an independent field of study and strove to have it recognized as an academic discipline on its own right, Max Weber, had in 1890 only just got his doctors degree in law, but soon embarked on the study of agrarian conditions east of the Elbe which led him into considerations on the relationship between economic values and other values.

The fifth of the sociological pioneers relevant in this connection, Vilfredo Pareto, at that time was still an Italian engineer and amateur economist, but in 1893 he mooved to Lausanne where next year he became the successor of Léon Walras. Only around 1900 had he arrived at the conviction that the râtional side of man supposed by economists to reign supreme in large areas of social life is less important that the irrational side, and only in 1916 was he able to present his sociology as the theory of the "non-logical" in his majestic *Trattato di sociologia generale* (English: The Mind and Society 1935).

The concept of value plays different roles in the works of these pioneers, but for most of them it is an important role. And for most of them the need for a science like that which Comte had christened "sociology" arose from dissatisfaction with the onesidedness of the only mature social scientific theory extant, neo-classical (marginalist) economics.[69] Durkheim is to some extent an exception. He was more interested in showing the insufficiency of psychological explanations of social phenomena than in critizising the economists, although he certainly found that what they had to say on e.g. the division of labour was in need of decisive complementation. He was, of course, extremely interested in questions of morals, but in his treatment of these questions the concept of value is less important than the related concept of social norm. For this reason the following account will be limited to the other four pioneers.

It would not be quite correct to say that while "value" was employed by the economists to express an aspect of rational choice, the sociologists used the term to stress irrational factors in human conduct. The sociologists did not generally tend to endorse a Dionysian against an Apollonian view. But when they emphasized the role of values in human affairs they had the importance of religious, moral and social constraints on individual choices in mind. Against some tendencies in previous social thought of importance for the development of economic theory they claimed that social life would not be possible if a conception of man as always seeking the best means to further his own narrow interests were correct.[70]

XI

One way to approach the question of "value" in the works of turn-of-the-century sociologists is to study Max Weber's inaugural lecture from 1895 *Der Nationalstat und die Volkswirtschaftspolitik*,[71] in which he refers to the abovementioned investigations of the agrarian conditions in Western Prussia, conducted for the "Verein für Sozialpolitik".[72] They had convinced him that economic conditions and policies like those in Prussian agriculture cannot be understood if only economic points of view are taken into consideration. He had found that the economic interest of the great landowners who dominated there – the Junkers – were in conflict with values connected with their German nationalism. Economic motives had led them to employ migrant Polish and Russian daylabourers who crossed the Eastern border, rather than German peasants hired on yearly contract as quasi-servile labour. The growing number af Slavs was felt as a threat to the unity and integrity of the German nation, and Bismarck – himself a Junker – had closed the frontier, but after his fall it had been reopened.

Weber drew the conclusion that a set of values like nationalism may be in conflict with other sets like economic ones. In the inaugural lecture, it is true, he expressed doubts whether economic values form a unique autonomous set; he said that it is an "optical illusion that there are autonomous economical ... ideals" and that "our science includes a chaos of value standards, some of eudaimonistic, some of ethical character".[73] In his later works, primarily *Wirtschaft und Gesellschaft* (*Economy and Society*), he to some extent embraced neoclassical economic theory and was more inclined to accept that statments of what is right or best from a purely economic point of view have meaning. But other points of view may lead to other results.

That non-economic values may influence economic life is of course also the point of his great works on religion and economics, which began with *Die protestantische Ethik und der 'Geist' des Kapitalismus* (*The Protestant Ethics and the Spirit of Capitalism*), published in 1905 in the *Archiv für Sozialwissenschaft und Sozialpolitik*, of which he had resumed co-editorship two years earlier. That values of different kinds are not only important as part of the reality which social science studies, but also enter into the scientific process itself is a main point in the methodological papers he published in the years from 1903 and which are collected in *Gesammelte Schriften zur Wissenschaftslehre*.[74]

We are here taught, on the one hand, that values necessarily enter into the process of concept formation in the cultural sciences, and on the other that the social sciences must be value-neutral. It is now generally accepted that in his methodological work Weber is indebted to the Neo-Kantian philosopher Heinrich Rickert (1863-1936) who was his collegue first in Freiburg and then in Heidelberg. In order to understand his use of the concept of value we have to look into Neo-Kantianism, even to go back to Immanuel Kant himself.

XII

In 1865 Otto Liebmann, a 25 year old German philosopher issued a book entitled *Kant und die Epigonen* (Kant and the Epigons),[75] in which each chapter ended with the words "Also muss auf Kant zurückgegangen werden" (Therefore we must return to Kant).[76] This became a battle cry for a number of other German philosophers who agreed with Liebmann that the development after Kant through Fichte, the Romantics and Hegel had led into a blind alley. It had created an unhealthy distance, not to say opposition, between science and philosophy; on the one hand the idealist philosophy had become anti-scientific, on the other a crude materialism paraded as the only world-view legitimized by science.

In this context to return to Kant meant to resume his endeavours to furnish a philosophical justification for the basic presuppositions of science and, at the same time, to delineate the boundary line between what can and what cannot be treated scientifically.

The science whose presuppositions Kant sought to justify was the one which for a century had been considered paradigmatic, Newtonian mechanics. To defend this science against Humean scepticism, while at the same time showing that a comparable defence cannot be delivered for speculative metaphysical theories, was at least a major part of Kant's purpose. A main feature of the scientific revolution of the 17th century which culminated in the Newtonian synthesis was the application of mathematics to the physical world. One of Kant's tasks was, accordingly, to justify the applicability of mathematical theories, which seemed the result of pure reasoning, to the real world to which access seems to be through experience. This question had been a bone of contention between rationalists and empiricists. The Kantian critical philosophy represents a junction where these two lines of 17th and 18th century philosophy meet and from which new lines which marks 19th century thought issue.

The means by which Kant defended mathematical physics was the idea that our experience of reality is conditioned by the applicability of forms of intuition ("Anschauungsformen") and of understanding ("Verstandsformen, Kategorien") to the manifold delivered by the senses. The validity of the propositions in which the essences of these forms are expressed, including the propositions of mathematics and the principle of causality, is guaranteed by the fact that that which does not fit into the forms is rejected as unreal. A comparable validation of the metaphysical concepts ("Vernunftformen, Ideen") of God, The World as a Whole, and The Soul cannot be given, since they transcend experience. The various proofs of the existence of God are invalid, and the use of these concepts leads to antinomies.

This, however, is only one side of the matter. Reason has not only a theoretical aspect; there is also a practical reason which tells us what our duty is, and since the concept of duty would be meaningless if there were no just retribution in an afterlife, we must postulate the existence of immortal souls and a God who is just and omnipotent. We also have to postulate freedom of the will. But all attempts to determine the content of the rules of duty from a conception of God as our creator and master fail, as do all attempts to deduce them from facts about human nature. Any attempt of this kind results in a heteronomous ethics incompatible with the essential character of morals as autonomous. Morality is a question of what is our duty and has nothing to do with our inclinations or our striving for happiness. The criteria for what is our duty which reason gives are purely formal.

Kant's position has often been expressed as that of separating "sein" (existence, fact) and "sollen" (ought, duty, value) absolutely. This, in my opinion, is one of the two aspects of his philosophy which through Neo-Kantianism came to influence Max Weber and other sociologists strongly. The second aspect is the idea that it is the forms or concepts which human cognitive faculties apply in experiencing reality that determine this reality. The Neo-

Kantians, however, found a major difficulty in Kants's development of this idea. This difficulty he himself had not been unaware of, and already some of his contemporaries had claimed it to be unsurmountable. In describing experience as the result of a synthesis of a given manifold effected by the forms of intuition and understanding Kant suggested that the material for this synthesizing process originated from a transcendent, noumenal reality, the thing-in-itself. But we cannot know this thing-in-itself, and to see it as the origin of the material out of which the phenomenal world is construed means to apply the category of causality outside of experence, which is illegitimate, since its validity has only been proved within experience. Kant therefore emphasizes that we can only have a negative concept or a limiting concept ("Grenzbegriff") of the noumenal reality, which we nevertheless have to presuppose to give meaning to the concept of the phenomenal reality, the experienced reality. We cannot characterize it positively in any way. But to confer reality and causal efficacy to it is to characterize it positively.

Now, in order to account for the freedom of the will Kant has to distinguish between the self that belongs to the phenomenal, causally ordered world and a noumenal self. And in the third Critique (*Kritik der Urteilskraft*) he points out some experiences (from the field of aesthetics and that of natural teleology) which point to a connection between the noumenal self which is the bearer of the apriori forms and the noumenal realm from which the material of our experiences originates. In this way he suggests the possibility of breaking down some of the main distinctions of his philosophy, a possibility which his successors used in developing idealistic philosophies. In these they thought that the difficulty mentioned above disappeared, but even if this is correct – which the Neo-Kantians denied – new difficulties arose.

When the young Otto Liebmann declared all post-Kantian German philosophy misdirected he maintained, on the one hand, that its main lines of development all originated in Kant's criticism, on the other hand he pointed out the abovementioned difficulty and blamed "the epigones" for having either neglected it or presented invalid solutions to it. It would take us too far from our main topic to discuss to what extent Liebmann was right in his criticism of "the epigones"; the important thing is that nearly all of the Neo-Kantians agree with him that the idea of a thing-in-itself as a reality "behind" the appearances had to be abolished from Kants's philosophy and that with this modification it embodied the only fruitful approach to the problem of justifying the presuppositions of the existing scientific theories.

Liebmann certainly underestimated the degree to which this modification would interfere with the parts of Kant's philosophy which had been developed in the second and third Critiques (*Kritik der praktischen Vernunft*, *Kritik der Urteilskraft*), and the Neo-Kantians had to make major reconstructions to make whole philosophical systems out of what they conceived as the kernel of Kant's teaching. Such reconstructions may be made in various directions, and we in fact find a great variety of Neo-Kantian philosophies in the last third of the 19th century and the beginning of the 20th. What unites the Neo-Kantians, in addition to their dependence on Kant, is perhaps best expressed negatively: they reacted not only against the idealism of Hegel and others, but also against positivism as represented by Comte and Mill, and they finally rejected all kinds of psychologism, including psychologistic interpretations of Kant.

XIII

This last point is particularly prominent in the so-called Marburg-school, represented in our period by Hermann Cohen (1842-1918) and Paul Natorp (1854-1924). They accepted Kant's conception of the justification of science – in particular mathematics and mathematical physics – as a primary task of philosophy. Like Liebmann they departed from Kant in critizising the concept of the thing-in-itself. Cohen denied the existence of a real noumenal world and reinterpreted the thing-in-itself as a methodological idea which indicates the progressive direction of knowledge. The Marburg philosophers did not envisage a science of society.[77] To Cohen and Natorp the intellectual grasp of society was part of the work of practical reason; it was not a question of finding and describing the structure of a social reality, but of clarifying the ideal of a just society. This was the basis of the influential jurisprudence of Rudolf Stammler (1856-1938), whom Max Weber critizised so vehemently.[78]

The other main school of Neo-Kantianism, the Baden or Southwest German school, is much more important in this context since it was more interested in the human sciences – at that time called "Geisteswissenschaften" or "Kulturwissenschaften" in Germany. This is the school to which Rickert belonged, together with his teacher Wilhelm Windelband (1848-1915). Windelband's name is linked to the introduction of the terms "nomothetic" and "idiographic" for the two kinds of science which are distinguished by their different aims, the first kind being engaged in finding general laws, the second in describing and explaining concrete particulars. History is the idiographic science par excellence; Windelband may therefore with his distinction be said to have entered the vivid discussion about the nature of historical knowledge which took place in Germany through most of the 19th century. The questions whether there are specific historical laws (laws of social development), whether there are timeless laws for social life of the same logical structure as natural laws, and whether a faculty of "Einfühlung" (empathy) plays a necessary role in historical understanding, were debated as part of the attack on Hegelianism, the debates of Marxism, and the battle between the historical school and the marginalists in economics (the socalled "Methodenstreit"). These debates are all of importance as a background for the methodological work of Max Weber.

As regards Windelband it ought to be mentioned that he agreed with Liebmann and the Marburg philosophers that turning back to Kant also meant transcending him by eliminating the dual-reality idea. In a speech on the occasion of the centennial of the publication of the first Critique (*Kritik der reinen Vernunft*) he claimed that the idea of a noumenal world behind the phenomenal one is a remnant of the error of conceiving knowledge as consisting of depicting or mirroring an independently existing reality, an error which otherwise it is Kant's great merit to be the first to expose.[79] Windelband interprets Kant as basing his epistemology on the concept of rules; truth is not a question of correspondence of ideas with objects, but of mutual relations between ideas in accordance with a priori given rules. An experienced object is a combination of ideas according to the rules which express the content of the a priori forms. We cannot and we need not know whether anything exists behind it.

In the fields of ethics and aesthetics, too, everything depends on rules. Here it is the will, respectively the emotions, which must correspond to rules. The task of philosophy, according to Windelband, is to make explicit the rules or norms which confer validity and value to our thought, will, and emotions. Truth, as he develops further in his paper "What is philosophy?", is a kind of value, and philosophy is the science of the universal values.[80]

It has been pointed out that both main branches of Neo-Kantianism were influenced by Rudolf Hermann Lotze, who had been Windelband's teacher. Lotze (1817-1881) developed a system in which "validity" (Geltung) and "value" (Wert) are the central notions. In addition to a world of necessarily valid truths, which are independent of whether we experience any objects to which their contents refer, there are facts given in perception, and finally there is a world of values. We have a reason "sensitive to values" (Wertempfindende Vernunft), which i.a. recognizes acts of will as morally good or bad. Lotze, who also influenced the Austrian philosophers of value – he was instrumental in getting Brentano the chair in Vienna – was important for the introduction of value as the central notion in practical philosophy. This is not in accordance with Kant for whom duty was the central notion, but it influenced many who in other respects were followers of Kant, not the least Windelband and Rickert. It must, however, be admitted that there are suggestions in the second Critique, in particular in a chapter entitled "Vom Begriffe eines Gegenstandes der reinen praktischen Vernunft" (On the concept of an object of the pure practical reason),[81] of how moral goodness may be considered a species of goodness, parallel to the pleasant ("das angenehme") and the useful ("das nützliche"). The last mentioned concepts are nevertheless dependent upon human desires and inclinations, while it is the pure practical reason which determines the morally good. When the sharp Kantian distinction between "sein" and "sollen" is sometimes translated into that between fact and value, this is misleading, since the pleasant and the useful belong to the world of facts, according to Kant.

Within the Lotzean framework of "validity" and "value", the question of validity may be given priority over that of value -this points in the direction of the Marburg school – or vice versa, as in the Baden school. Heinrich Rickert was among those who developed a general theory of value in continuation of Windelband's placing values in the center of philosophical enquiry.

XIV

Before we look into Rickert's theory of value we must consider the theory of concept formation in the human sciences which he developed in his great work on the limits of natural scientific concept formation.[82] Max Weber read it when it came out in 1902 and wrote to his wife: "Rickert is very good". He continued: "To a very large extent I find in this book what I have thought myself, although in logically untreated form".[83] Already in the article he published in the *Archiv* in 1904 as a declaration of his editorial policy he gives an account of concept formation in the cultural sciences which is in nearly complete agreement with that af Rickert.[84] Both presuppose a 'hiatus irrationalis' between concepts and reality – in typically Neo-Kantian manner.

Reality is concrete, individual, qualitatively characterized. And it is infinite in the sense that no exhaustive description can be given, even of the smallest part of it; a network of concepts can never catch all details. In order to create scientific knowledge one has to select and abstract. In natural science the principle of selection is given by the aim of finding universally valid laws. This is not the aim of the human sciences, so another principle is needed here. In these sciences which deal with cultural phenomena the interest lies in understanding the cultural meaning (Sinn) of the individual phenomena. To grasp this we have to relate them to values. So both Rickert and Weber emphasize the role of "Wertbeziehungen" (value relevances) in concept formation in these sciences. Weber distinguishes between the subjective meaning which the actors in whom we are interested attach to their conduct and the artifacts they work with on the one hand, and the cultural meaning defined by the generally accepted interests of the investigator on the other. It is the latter which is determined by relations to generally accepted values, but nothing can have cultural meaning without having subjective meaning.

That values enter is due to the fact that they determine what we regard as essential, important, and significant; in designating something "cultural" we imply that it is significant and is related to general values. It does not have to be valuable in the sense of having positive value; the opposite may be the case and the reason why we are interested in understanding it.[85] As appears from the title of Weber's paper on "objectivity" he is concerned with the objectivity of social scientific knowledge. And for Rickert the main point of his great work is to show that historical investigations of all kinds may constitute objective science. But here one should think that the value relevance is an obstacle. The result of an investigation of a cultural phenomenon seems to depend on which value we choose to refer it to and therefore not to have universal validity.[86]

XV

Rickert, however, argues that to establish value relevance is not the same as to evaluate, and Weber, who is famous for his thesis of the value-neutrality of science, of course agrees. As Rickert expresses it: "If the connection of value to object is essential to historical science without compromising its objectivity, that is ... because objects can be related to values in a purely theoretical fashion without thereby valuating these objects as deserving of praise or blame".[87] Weber conceives the relationship between valuations and value relevances in the light of his theory of increasing rationality.[88] The domain of values is rationalized by a process of intellectualization in which values are articulated and detached from their emotional and volitional origins.

This may or may not be correct, but even if value relevances are in this way independent of valuations, the possibility of choice between different values seems to introduce a kind of relativism, not easily reconciled with scientific objectivity.

Here Rickert answers that the choice is not free, but bound by certain requirements. In history we deal with persons, their conduct and their products, and we must respect the valuations involved on their part.[89] Secondly the values chosen must not be personal or private; they must express general concerns of a culture. Finally these general cultural values must have objective validity.[90]

Here the theory of value, which Rickert only developed fully in 1913 in a paper in *LOGOS*[91] and particularly in his *System der Philosophie* from 1921,[92] is presupposed. Rickert there introduces a distinction between the real and the non-real ("das Irreale").[93] A spoken sentence is not only physical sounds and thoughts in the minds of the speaker and listener, it also has "Sinn", meaning, which is something "irreales".[94] Truth and falsity are value qualities of such meanings – nowadays often called propositions. To express the positive characteristics of what has at first only been characterized negatively as the non-real two terms may be used. They are "Wert" (value) and "Geltung" (validity).[95] All values have validity,[96] but one must distinguish between a wider and a narrower concept of validity.

A feeling of pleasure is an evaluative act, and every such act presupposes or constitutes a value. But the validity of such a value concerns only the person who has the pleasure, it is only subjective validity.[97] The narrower concept of validity is an objective one; it entails a "sollen". A true sentence has such objective validity; everybody "soll" accept it.[98] Truth for Rickert is the paradigmatic objective value; its value can be proved by the selfcontradictions which arise if it is denied.[99] But also other values, e.g. ethical ones, have objective validity, although this cannot be proven in this way.[100] Between these two kinds of validity Rickert recognizes a third: that of general acceptance.[101]

Theories which try to include values which depend on individual or collective attitudes of approval or disapproval and objective values under one concept run into trouble.[102] We saw that this was the case with the philosophies of value of the Austrians. Rickert tries to solve such problems by taking the difference between subjective and objective values to be analogous to the distinction between appearance and reality.[103] But this won't do! The subjective value caviar may have for me is not a more or less misleading appearance of its real value. Rickert may have felt this; at least he did not go much further into subjective values, but concentrated on the objective ones for which he developed a classification. He thought it possible by employing only formal critieria to find "übergeschichtliche Faktoren" (timeless factors) and establish a system, an ordering, even a rank ordering, which makes it possible to "die Werte gegeneinander abzuschätzen" (to make values commensurable).[104] In a very artificial manner, which I shall not go further into, he arrived at a sixfold classification: logical, aesthetic, ethical, personal and two kinds of religious values.[105] Each of these classes of value delineates and governs a certain cultural sphere: science, art, morality, that of personal relations, in particular love relations, and religion in its two main forms. It is however not clear how a rank order between them is established.

XVI

Weber did not develop a theory of value like that of Rickert, and he did not consider truth to be a value – although a true belief of course may be of value to the believer. He therefore really had no answer to the question whether the necessary value relevance does not jeopardise the objectivity of the cultural sciences.[106] He may have thought of the main cultural values as something objectively given, but at least he was very emphatic that they are incommensurable. This insight had been growing on him since his investigations of Prussian agriculture and had become a central point in his worldview. It meant a definite limit to what reason and rationality can achieve, as Roger Brubaker has elucidated in a study a few years ago.[107]

Let me quote some of his well-known expressions of this incommensurability. Weber states that "the different value orders in the World are engaged in an irreconcilable battle with each other",[108] that the battle is "like that between God and the devil",[109] so that "absolute polytheism is the only appropriate metaphysics of the world of value".[110] Weber denies that the ethical point of view is a superior one from which the struggle between other values may be decided; there are autonomous nonethical value spheres.[111] In the lecture on *Politik als Beruf* (Politics as a Vocation) which he gave in München in 1918 Weber mentions politics as an example of this. In politics other rules apply than the ethical rules concerned with salvation of souls. The politician must look to the results of his efforts and may have to use morally doubtful means. He must have dealings with diabolical powers and cannot follow an ethics of charity.[112]

Weber's presentations of these matters are scattered and very unsystematic and there has been much debate on their interpretation. There is, however, no reason to doubt that H.H.Bruun is right in claiming that this incompatibility and incommensurability between diffent values or spheres of value for Weber is a principle of logic and not a contingent fact.[113] That the Kantian distinction between "sein" and "sollen" forms the background of the principle, and that it is closely connected with the doctrine of the "Wertfreiheit" (often translated as value-neutrality) of science is also indisputable. How this doctrine is to be understood in detail, and what kind of support Weber has given it – or thought he had given it – is less clear. He may have been aware of the ambiguities of the term "value", but he seems not to have distinguished between conflicts and incommensurabilities on different levels. Whereas Turner and Factor have pointed out that not only first-order conflicts between substantive values, but also second-order conflicts between alternative theories of justification of first-order values are involved,[114] Roger Brubaker claims that Weber confuses clashes between value-orientations and clashes between value-spheres.[115] "Value-orientation" is a translation of Weber's "Weltanschauung", while Weber's term "Wertsphäre" has been translated literally.

The idea that socio-cultural life falls into a number of spheres like religion, morals, politics, economics, art, etc., each organized around a central value or set of values is common to Rickert, Weber, and, as we shall see, Simmel.

That Weber was always on guard against attempts to blur the distinction between the factual and the normative and to deduce practical consequences from purely factual knowledge is exemplified in his attack on Rudolf Stammler (see note 78). He not only accused Stammler of basing his defence of the materialist conception of history on a quite erroneous presupposition concerning causal explanations – that if such an explanation is to be valid it is necessary to subsume all events under one law, to point to one causal factor which lies behind everything. He also shows how Stammler plays on ambiguities in words like "law", "rule", "material", and "nature" to blur crucial distinctions as that between a factual regularity (a "sein") and a norm (a "soll"). Weber finds this particularly blameworthy in someone who "wants to be recognized as the most genuine pupil of Kant"[116] – Stammler, as mentioned above, belonged to the Marburg school.

XVII

Georg Simmel (1858-1918) was a philospher as well as a sociologist. He lived most of his life in Berlin where he studied and taught at the university[117] – he was a brilliant lecturer – and kept a kind of "salon" where many members of the artistic and intellectual elite, including Rickert and Weber, met.[118] He was a Kantian, but did not belong to any of the dominant Neo-Kantian schools.

Like other Neo-Kantians he had misgivings concerning the thing-in-itself. In *Einleitung in die Moralwissenschaft* (Introduction to the Science of Morality) (1892-93) he states that there are not two realities, a phenomenal and a noumenal one, but only one reality which can be imagined in two ways. Kant is misunderstood if we take the distinction between appearances and the thing-in-itself as a metaphysical one; what he really wanted was to teach us that all our knowledge is bound to sense impressions as its material and that pure reason cannot give us knowledge of a reality beyond these.[119]

Simmel is also a Kantian in the sense that he emphasizes the active role of our cognitive faculties in forming the experienced reality. His theory of concept formation in the human sciences was first set forth in *Die Probleme des Geschichtsphilosophie* (The Problems of the Philosophy of History) (1892). It is rather like those of Rickert and Weber.[120] Like these Simmel emphasizes "the distance between experience and its theoretical construct". He supports "the thesis that no science can completely express the complexity and the qualitatively infinite profusion of real existence", but maintains that "even if a qualitatively and quantitatively complete description of reality were possible" it would not constitute scientific knowledge.[121] What is lacking is "a point of view or problematic". "Such a problematic is necessary in order to produce a construct that would satisfy our criteria for knowledge".[122] It is a task for the philosophy of history to specify the point of view which is peculiar to history, to ask what makes an event a historical event. Simmel explicitly compares his analysis with Kant's analysis of the presuppositions of natural science,[123] and as Kant may be said to expose the errors of naive realism, Simmel views the purpose of his book to be to combat historical realism, i.e. the position that historical knowledge is possible in so far as it constitutes a mirror image of the events as they actually happened. There are important differences between natural science and history, but "every form of knowledge represents a translation of immediately given data into a new language, a language with its own intrinsic forms, categories, and requirements".[124]

Here we meet the key concept in Simmel's whole philosophy: form. As he himself has stated in an autobiographical fragment, he found the form-content (form-material) relationship within epistemology, but developed it into a methodological principle in the various sciences.[125] He used it e.g. to distinguish sociology from the other social sciences by its focusing on the forms of sociation, while these deal with various kinds of content.[126] Those who have critizised Simmel for using "form" in many different senses are probably right, but the importance of the notion in his philosophy clearly has to do with his dependence on Kant's philosophy.

But how do the various sciences choose the forms by which they structure their object? Simmel is not as explicit on the role of values in this connection as Rickert and Weber, but he emphasizes – under the influence of the evolutionist and pragmatist currents of his time – the dependence of knowledge on action, and there are suggestions in his works of the position that practical interests determine the problematics which determine the forms to be used.

This does not mean that he rejects or neglects the Kantian distinction between "sein" and "sollen". His *Einleitung* begins with a account of "sein" and "sollen" as "original categories", and he states that we can only prove logically the we "soll" something by tracing it back to another "sollen" presupposed as valid.[127] In the beginning of *The Philosophy of Money*[128] he declares that independently of "the order in which things are placed as natural entities" when we confer existence and causal connections on them, there is another order in which we arrange them – "an order of value". And "the value of objects, thoughts and events can never be inferred from their mere natural existence and content".[129] Neither existence, nor value, are qualities, they are forms in which what Simmel calls "Lebensinhalte" are ordered.[130]

The book on the philosophy of money is Simmel's masterpiece. He had for a long time been interested in the phenomenon of money and its role in modern life.[131] Money, in addition to being of great social importance, was of interest to him as the purest possible case of something the essence of which lies wholly in its relationships and which therefore has no quality, only quantity. He was aware of the role of the concept of value in economic theory, and although his intention was not to write an economic treatise he felt it necessary to start the book with a sketch of a theory of value. This, however, proved difficult for him. In a letter to Rickert of May 1895 he complained that he found it very hard without giving up his fundamental relativism to do justice to the claims to recognition which absolute and objective values actually make.[132] It is doubtful whether he really solved this problem.

In chapter 1 of *Philosophie des Geldes* he admits that values are usually experienced as subjective, not as something adhering to objects as e.g. colours and temperature. But he adds that the exceptions are the interesting cases.[133] This leads him to look into the relationship between subject and object, also in the theoretical sphere. He advances the theory that the primitive form of experience is a unitary one, the distinction between the experienced object and the experiencing subject being a product of a development, in the individual as well as in the culture.[134] In aesthetic experience the original unity is approached, and, in general, when we enjoy something we do not distinguish between the enjoyment and that which we enjoy. Only when obstacles prevent us from enjoyments, and desires therefore arise, do we experience value as connected to the objects of desire.[135] Even though value-experience involves subjective elements like sentiment and desire its ideal content may in this way be objectified.

The question of validity ("Gültigheit"), however, concerns a third category. This is so in cognition, where concepts like triangle, causality, and gravitation have their own validity, independent of whether they are realized in space or in consciousness.[136] Analogously, values may have validity independently of whether anybody appreciates them. This according to Simmel applies to moral values and "all the way down to the economic values ascribed to objects which are traded on the market".[137] A valid value has a special relation to a subject – it claims to be recognized.[138] Such claims are experienced within the subject and have no counterpart in the objects themselves. They can be traced neither to the subject, nor to the object. Values which in this way claim recognition belong to a metaphysical category; they stand above the subject-object dualism, just as the unitary immediate enjoyment "stands below" this dualism.[139]

Simmel explicitly denies that all values are of this kind: "The metaphysical sublimation of values does not play any role in the valuations of daily life".[140] Among these are those of exchangeable goods, so the expression "all the way down to" (hinunter bis zu) used above must be taken to mean "down to, but not including". Economic values are, however, objectified by the market mechanisms which bestow prices on the various objects of exchange.

What Simmel has to say about economic value and money, including the social and personal consequences of the introduction of increasingly pure forms of money, makes up the greater part of the work and is of great psychological and sociological interest. My short report on the theory of value in the first chapter does not do justice to the subtlety of Simmel's thought, and I am not sure that I have not misunderstood some points, but it seems to me that he has not really explained how some values have validity and others not.

The questions of how values fall into different kinds and of whether these are commensurable are not treated explicitly in the first chapter. Two things may, however, be said on these points. One is that Simmel, like Rickert and Weber, takes moral life, art, science, religion, etc. to be spheres of life ("Welten") each of which is governed by a particular kind of value as "Organizationsprinzip".[141] The second is that money seems to be a means by which values are made commensurable. But there are limits to this. Simmel e.g. shows this when he treats of prostitution. He states that in our culture – in contradistinction to some other cultures which take a quite different attitude towards prostitution – there is "total incommensurability" between money and "female sexual honour".[142] Since prostitution is a fact also in our culture, it might be said that these values have been compared in some cases and a choice made. But this does not mean that they have been made commensurable, since, as Weber would have emphasized, the choice can hardly be called a rational one.

XVIII

The efforts by the pioneers to have sociology recognized as an independent academic subject were not immediately successful. Durkheim's chair at the Sorbonne was only changed from one in the theory of education to one in sociology five years before his death, and in most other European universities it took much longer to establish such chairs.[143] But research institutes and sociological societies grew up already before World War I. In Germany such a society was planned in 1908 when Ferdinand Tönnies (1855 -1931) visited Max Weber in Heidelberg. They invited Simmel to join them and he became the first main speaker at the first meeting of the German Sociological Association in Frankfurt 1910.[144] Simmel left the executive committee of the association in 1913. Max Weber, although for a few years heavily engaged in the leadership of the association, was also active in "Verein für Sozialpolitik". At meetings in both associations he defended his thesis of the "Wertfreiheit" of science. At a meeting of the "Verein" in 1909 he did so in such a provocative manner that it created quite an uproar.[145] As a result of this he prepared a memorandum on the question for a closed meeting of the "Verein". The result of the discussion of this meeting which took place in Vienna in January 1914 was that he left the "Verein". The memorandum forms the basis for the important paper *Der Sinn der "Wertfreiheit" der soziologischen und ökonomischen Wissenschaften*.[146]

While Simmel did not take part in the debate,[147] Tönnies, on the contrary, supported Weber's position in a criticism of Troeltsch, in which he stressed the necessity of "keeping practical aspirations, whatever their aim, stricly separate from scientific thinking and research".[148] On the relation between Tönnies and Weber it may be emphasized that the latter admired *Gemeinschaft und Gesellschaft*, Tönnies' classic work, and that they agreed that the two key concepts in the title were examples of ideal-type concepts, although Tönnies originally used the term "normal concepts".[149] He was intersted in questions of concept formation in the social sciences and considered his main concepts – including "Naturwille" and "Kürwille" – as thought products, "tools devised in order to facilitate the understanding of reality". He admonished his readers that "the artificial, even forced, character of these abstractions must always be kept clearly in mind".[150] But there is nothing in his conception of concept formation like the value relevance thesis of Rickert and Weber, and the value concept is not prominent in his work.

Vilfredo Pareto (1848-1923), the last of the sociological pioneers introduced in section X, approached the concept of value in a manner typical of economists after the marginalist revolution. These in general followed Menger in ascribing intrinsic value to the pleasurable state of mind produced by the satisfaction of a need or a wish, but they introduced the word "utility" for this satisfaction considered as a quantity, despite the fact that it really refers to a property of instrumentally valuable, useful things. For this and other reasons Pareto coined a new term "ophelimity" for "the individual's satisfaction" of which the individual "is the only judge".[151] He continued, however, to use the term utility, and was not really consistent in his terminology. Raymond Aron has pointed out that ophelimity need not be the same as pleasure. My wish may be to conform to a social norm or to further some ideal, rather than to obtain pleasure.[152] The utility or ophelimity of different individuals are heterogenous quantities, but if we keep within the boundaries of economic theory we need not presuppose that they are measurable. Since we cannot add quantities of ophelimity from different individuals the only meaning we can give to the term "maximum ophelimity for a community" is a state where the ophelimity of none of its members can be increased without that of some others being diminished[153]. A community is not like an individual, but we can talk of the ophelimity of a community. This however, presupposes that we arbitrarily stipulate which quality is relevant: military power, economic prosperity, national glory, or what have you.[154]

By going beyond purely economic considerations we may also, according to Pareto, introduce criteria according to which some distribution of economic goods is to be preferred to others. This gives a sociological concept of the maximum of ophelimity for a community. The criteria then select one among those states which have maximal economic ophelimity for the community.[155] But again, the choice of the criteria is arbitrary.

The main point in all this is that if value is identified with ophelimity, values for different individuals are incommensurable. This is another type of incommensurability than the one Weber and Simmel maintained, but Pareto and Weber agree that we can only prove a prescriptive judgment on the basis of another prescriptive judgment, and that basic prescriptive principles are matters of arbitrary stipulation, or, as Parto puts it, of "non-experimental hypotheses".[156]

XIX

It would, of course, have been possible to add more turn-of-the-century philosophers and sociologists to those who, in the previous pages, have been used to exemplify the great interest in values in the period in question.[157] The survey given is, however, comprehensive enough, I think, to demonstrate the points made in the first sections: that this interest was connected with the development in economic theory, that the Kantian "sein-sollen" distinction formed an important background for some, and that the term value was used both in the context of theories of rational choice and to emphasize religious, moral and legal constraints on such choices and even to do justice to more irrational sources of human behaviour.

In addition to these points the survey has shown how many difficulties the ambiguities of the term value have created. Some of the necessary distinctions have been pointed out in the course of the survey, but at least one has to be added. It has been expressed by the sociologist Allen Barton in terms of "values as attributes of people" versus "values as attributes of objects". Barton explains it as follows: "There are ... two things involved in any discussion about values: the objects which are valued, and the tendency or standard within the person to behave in certain ways toward these objects".[158] On the one hand, then, we have the object valued (often called the value) and the property attributed to it in the valuation, on the other the standard employed. To this one might, with Nicholas Rescher, add "the locus of value", that is the properties of the object which is the basis for its being attibuted a value of a certain kind and degree according to the standard.[159] Rescher is among those philosophers who, after the period we have been concerned with, have used modern methods of analysis to eliminate some of the obscurities and ambiguities in value theory. Another is Everett W. Hall, who in his *What is Value?* made an analysis which may be said to continue the work of the late Brentano and the younger generation of Brentaneans.[160] In an introductory lecture on problem formation at a seminar on "Conceptions of values and the development of value systems" I have drawn on the work of such philosophers and social scientists to present the state of value theory some years ago.[161]

An important question which has been dealt with in several places in the previous sections is whether the idea of considering economic values, ethical values, aesthetic value, etc. as different species of a common genus, value in general, has proved to be fruitful, and whether these different kinds of value are commensurable. I have come to the conclusion that the idea in question is not really tenable, and that there are several reasons for denying commensurability.

Notes

1. The most conspicuous expression of this attitude was perhaps the special issues in 1919 of Karl Kraus' "Die Fackel" entitled *Die letzten Tage der Menschheit*.
2. See e.g. Malcolm Bradbury and J. McFarlane, eds.: *Modernism 1890-1930*, Harmondsworth 1976 and Irving Howe, ed.: *The Idea of the Modern in Literature and the Arts*. N. York 1967.
3. Among the many studies of the Viennese turn-of-the-century the following have been particularly useful for the work on this paper: Hermann Broch: *Hugo von Hofmannsthal and his Time. The European Imagination 1860-1920*. Transl., ed., and with an introd. by Michael P. Steinberg. Univ. of Chic. Press 1984. Allan Janik & Stephen Toulmin: *Wittgenstein's Vienna*. Simon and Schuster, New York 1973. William J. McGrath: *Dionysian Art and Populist Politics in Austria*. Yale Univ, Press, New Haven 1974. Carl E. Schorske: *Fin-de-siècle Vienna. Politics and Culture*. Knopf, N. York 1980. *Traum und Wirklichkeit. Wien 1870-1930*. Katalog: 93. Sonderausstellung des Historischen Museums der Stadt Wien ... 28. März bis 6. Oktober 1985 (Catalogue).
4. See William J. McGrath: *Dionysian Art...*,Ch 1. McGrath points out that the kernel of this group had graduated from the Benedictine Schottengymnasium. He is particularly interested in the connection between Gustav Mahler and Victor Adler within this context.
5. See McGrath *op. cit.* pp. 69 & 89.
6. See *Traum und Wirklichkeit*, pp. 18-21.
7. It may interest Danish readers that Harald Høffding visited Jodl in the summer 1896 at his cottage in Bohemia. In his memoirs (*Erindringer*, p. 179) Høffding relates that the two philosophers during long walks found that they agreed on many points, except on the religious question. Jodl maintained that Feuerbach had dealt conclusively with this question, while Høffding still saw unsolved psychological and ethical problems here. Høffding expresses admiration for Jodl's history of ethics, while Jodl, on the other hand, wrote a very appreciative review of Høffdings treatise on ethics (*Etik*, 1887).
8. The connections between what has been called the first Austrian school of value theory (Menger and his pupils) and the second school (Brentano, Meinong, v. Ehrenfels) has been treated in several contributions to the collective work entitled *Austrian Economics: Historical and Philosophical Background*, published in 1986 under the joint editorship of Wolfgang Grassl and Barry Smith.
9. In his *Selbstdarstellung* (in the first volume of the series "Philosophie der Gegenwart in Selbstdarstellungen", 2. Aufl. 1923) Meinong suggests that this was "nicht ohne Gewinn" for his later work in value theory (p. 103).
10. Adam Smith: *An Inquiry into the Nature and Causes of the Wealth of Nations* (1776) Book 1, Ch. 4. In the following this work will be quoted as WN.
11. *Id. loc.*
12. "The value of any commodity, therefore, to the person who possesses it, and who means not to use or consume it himself, but to exchange it for other commodities, is equal to the quantity of labour which it enables him to purchase or commmand." WN Book I, Ch 5. Other relevant quotations from Smith's works, and a general account of the discussion concerning his theory of value may be found in my paper "Natural Law and Social Science", *Danish Yearbook of Philosophy* 19, 1982, 7-62, in particular on pages 42-52.
13. See again my paper in *Danish Yearbook* 19, where I refer to the works of Marion Bowley: *Studies in the History of Economic Theory before 1870* (London 1973) and Marc Blaug: *Economic Theory in Retrospect*, 1962) 3. ed. Cambr. 1978.
14. The letter is quoted in Gunnar Myrdal: *The Political Element in the Development in*

Economics, London 1953 (Swedish original 1930). Myrdal in this work deals in detail with the Ricardo-Malthus debate and with the whole development of the labour theory of value, including Marx's use of it. He claims that also Adam Smith believed that the labour embodied in a commodity is the right measure of its value, and that John Locke's natural right theory of property was the ideological basis for this belief.

15. Various terms have been use to mark this distinction such as primary-secondary, intrinsic-instrumental or end-value versus means-value. The distinction is not as simple as it looks, in particular when value is taken to range from the positive to the negative, but we need not in this connection to go into the difficulties in formulating it precisely. The distinction may not be exhaustive, see e.g. William Frankena: *Ethics* (1963) 2. ed. Prentice-Hall, N. J. 1973, p. 82.

16. On Gossen see e.g. E. Kauder: *A History of Marginal Utility Theory*, 1965, pp. 46-51. Danish readers may find his formulations of the laws in the anthology *Deres egne ord*. Udvalg og kommentar ved Mogens Boserup II, G.E.C.Gad, København 1972, pp. 158-59.

17. Mark Blaug is probably right in claiming that the important point was the introduction of the idea of "the marginal" rather than the revival of a utility conception of value (see his *Economic Theory in Retrospect* (1962) 3.ed. repr. Cambr. Univ. Press 1980, p. 322). The marginalist point of view soon proved applicable also on the supply side, and Alfred Marshall meant in his *Principles of Economics* from 1890 to have shown how the amount of labour and other factors of production required to produce a commodity together with the satisfaction obtainable from it determines its price, provided both are treated in a marginalist manner. For the pioneers, however, the demand side dominated, and it is their emphasis on values in use and their rejection of the labour theory of value which in my view was important for the philosophers who promoted the idea of a general theory of value.

18. "Die Nationalökonomen neigen zum Glauben, dass ein Ding ein Gut sei, weil es aus Gütern produziert ist. (Es ist) indess klar, dass in Wahrheit gerade das Umgekehrte der Fall ist: Man verwendet Güter zu einer Produktion, weil das Produkt ein Gut sein wird" Carl Menger: *Grundsätze der Volkswirtschaftslehre* (1871) 2. Ausg. Wien 1923, p. 27.

19. "Der Wert ist demnach nichts den Gütern Anhaftendes, keine Eigenschaft derselben ... (Der Wert) ist die Bedeutung, welche konkrete Güter für den wirtschaftenden Menschen dadurch erlangen, dass die letzteren in der Befriedigung ihrer Bedürfnisse von der Verfügung über die betreffende Güter abhängig zu sein sich bewusst sind..." Carl Menger *op. cit.* p. 108.

20. W. Stanley Jevons: *The Theory of Political Economy* (1871) p. 129-30, quoted from *Deres egne ord II*, p. 167.

21. Jevons *op. cit.* quoted from *Deres egne ord II*, p. 166.

22. On von Ehrenfels' life and work see various contributions to the work *Austrian Economics, Historical and Philosophical Background* (AE) referred to in note 8 as well as W. Grassl's introduction to the first volume of his *Philosophische Schriften*, published by Philosophia Verlag (Munich and Vienna) 1982, which contains his works in the theory of value (EW). I have also had access to what Barry Smith has written on "The Theory of value of Chr. v. Ehrenfels" in a collective volume: *Christian von Ehrenfels, Leben und Werke*, edited by Reinhard Fabian.

23. See EW 69 and AE 41.

24. It is H.O.Eaton who in his *The Austrian Philosophy of Value* from 1930 introduced these labels. See EW 3.

25. On the connections between the two "schools" see the beginning of the contribution by Fabian and Simons to AE (pp. 37-101), where it is maintained that also the philosophers influenced the economists.
26. See Barry Smith's contribution to AE pp. 1-36.
27. The point of taking judgments to form a special category is that a mere combination of ideas which the British empiricists and those psychologists who followed them took to make up a judgment, lacks the constitutive aspect of affirmation or denial. Meinong became famous for introducing "Annahme" (supposition, assumption) as a special category between idea and judgment.
28. "Wert schreiben wir denjenigen Dingen zu, welche wir entweder tatsächlich begehren, oder doch begehren würden, falls wir nicht von ihrer Existenz überzeugt wären. Der Wert eines Dinges ist seine Begehrbarkeit ... Je stärker wir ein Objekt begehren oder begehren würden, desto höheren Wert besitzt er für uns" EW 253. The English translation is by Barry Smith (*The Theory of Value of Christian von Ehrenfels*, p. 155).
29. "Ein Ding begehren heisst entweder die Existenz des Dinges begehren, oder seinen Besitz, in welch letzterem Falle das Begehren auch auf ein Sein, jedoch nicht des Dinges selbst, sondern der Verfügungsmöglichkeit über dasselbe, und zugleich auf ein Nichtsein, die Abwesenheit aller jene Verfügungsgewalt behindernde Störungen, gerichtet ist" EW 254. The English translation is by Barry Smith. On the same page the author remembers that values may also be negative, in which case it is the nonexistence of the object which is desired. As Barry Smith remarks (*The Theory of Value of Christian von Ehrenfels*, p. 155), the introduction of existence here is equivalent to the more modern conception of states of affairs as the real objects of valuations. Meinong tends in the same direction, but his notion of existence is more abstract (*op. cit.* p. 156).
30. See EW 260-61.
31. "Wert ist eine Beziehung zwischen einem Objekte und einem Subjekte, welche ausdrückt, dass das Subjekt das Objekt entweder tatsächlich begehrt oder doch begehren würde, falls es von dessen Existenz nicht überzeugt wäre" EW 261.
32. See e.g. Carl Menger: *Grundsätze* pp. 144 sqq. There are formulations here which suggest that the value really originates in the (marginal) satisfaction, not in the first order economic good as such. Fr. v. Wieser dealt with imputation in his *Ursprung des wirtschaftlichen Wertes* (1884). See Mark Blaug: *Economic Theory in Retrospect*, pp. 453-54.
33. Ralph Barton Perry, the author of one of the first treatises on the general theory of value in the English language (*General Theory of Value*, Harv. Univ. Press 1926) seems not to have seen this.
34. Also on this point R. B. Perry is in my opinion at fault.
35. Originally published in *Vierteljahrsschrift für wissenschaftliche Philosophie,* reprinted in EW 23-166.
36. See EW 29.
37. See EW 32.
38. See EW 31.
39. See EW 32 note 6.
40. See EW 32 sqq.
41. EW 407-588.
42. EW 427-28.
43. "Man könnte somit – in Anlehnung an die weit verbreitete utilitarisrische Ethik – sich versucht finden, die Gemeinnützlichkeit resp. -schädlichkeit direkt als bestimmendes Moment für die ethische Wertung zu betrachten" EW 435.

44. "Diese Einvände verlangen in der Tat eine beträchtliche Modifikation der utilitaristischen Auffassung – deren Grundtendenz jedoch immerhin beibehalten werden kann" EW 436.
45. See EW 448-49.
46. See EW 444.
47. "Darum wird die Anwendung der allgemeinen Prinzipien der Werttheorie auf die Erscheinungen des ethischen Handelns, Fühlens and Urteilens nicht bei allen Beurteilen widerstandslos sich vollziehen, sondern mannigfachen Einvänden ...begegnen" EW 86.
48. "... nicht an die actuelle Werthhaltung ist der Werth gebunden, sondern an die mögliche Werthhaltung ... Der Werth besteht sonach nicht im Werthgehalten-werden, sondern im Werthgehalten-werden-können unter Voraussetzung der erforderlichen günstigen Umstände. Ein Gegenstand hat Werth, sofern er die Fähigkeit hat, für den ausreichend Orientierten, falls dieser normal veranlagt ist, die tatsächliche Grundlage für ein Werthgefühl anzugeben." Meinong: *Psychologische-ethische Untersuchungen zur Werth-Theorie.* Graz 1895, p. 25.
49. See Meinong *op. cit.* pp. 27-30 (§10. Die beiden Relativitäten am Werthe.)
50. Hume, whom Meinong admired and had studied thoroughly, in section 9 of *Enquiry Concerning the Principles of Morals* emphasizes the impersonality of moral values in the following way: "When a man denominates another his enemy ... he is understood to ... express sentiments peculiar to himself ... But when he bestows on any man the epithets vicious or odious or depraved, he then ... expresses sentiments in which he expects all his audience to concur with him".
51. The book was published posthumously by A. Marty in Graz 1923.
52. "Sage ich vom Himmel einmal, er sei blau, ein andermal, er sei schön, so erscheint dem Himmel dadurch hier nicht minder eine Eigenschaft beigelegt als dort, und ist beim Erfassen der betreffenden Eigenschaft hier so gut ein Gefühl beteiligt wie dort eine Vorstellung, so liegt nichts so nahe als die Präsentation, die dort jedermann der Vorstellung beimisst, hier dem Gefühle zuzuschreiben." A. Meinong: *Über emotionale Präsentation.* Kais. Akademie der Wissenschaften in Wien, Philosophisch-historische Klasse, Sitzungsberichte. 183. Band, 2. Abhandlung, Wien 1917, p. 33.
53. See in particular pp. 33-35. On p. 35 Rodhe concludes his analysis with the words. "Es handelt sich um zwei völlig verschiedene Begriffe, bei den das Gemeinsame nur das Wort Wert ist." (It concerns two completely different concepts which only has the word value in common).
54. "Der Wert eines Objektes besteht in der Tatsache, dass ein Subjekt am Objekt Interesse nimmt, nehmen könnte oder vernünftiger Weise nehmen sollte" Meinong: "Für die Psychologie und gegen den Psychologismus in der allgemeinen Werttheorie." *LOGOS* III, 1912, quoted from Rodhe *op. cit.* p. 34.
55. It is of course interesting that Meinong here introduces a quite new concept "interest", which seems more like von Ehrenfels' desire than feelings, but I shall neglect this point.
56. I take it that it is not necessary to account here for Franz Brentano's checkered career, on which information can be found in most histories of philosophy. It may perhaps be useful to remind the reader of the Aristotelian background of his philosophy, including his theory of value.
57. Edited by Franziska Mayer-Hillebrand and published by A. Francke Verlag in Bern 1952.
58. The modern standard edition is that of Oskar Kraus, Felix Meiner's Philosophische Bibliothek 1934. An English translation (*The Origin of our Knowledge of Right and Wrong*) of this edition was published in 1969 by Routledge & Kegan Paul. I refer to this work by U and a §-number, which can be found in both the German and the English version.

59. U § 23, 29-30.
60. U § 24.
61. U §§ 33-34.
62. U § 35.
63. This theory of truth has been put forward in Bretano's *Wahrheit und Evidenz*, first published in 1930, English translation in 1966. A summary is given in chapter 4 of R.M.Chisholm: *Brentano and Intrinsic Value*. Cambridge Univ. Press 1986. Chisholm on pp. 39 sqq. points out some grave difficulties in Brentano's theory.
64. See e.g. the letter to Oskar Kraus, U note to § 25.
65. U appendix XI § 13.
66. U § 22.
67. See Oskar Kraus: *Die Werttheorien. Geschichte und Kritik*. Verlag Rudolf M. Rohrer, Brünn 1937, p. 174.
68. Apart from the point about the law of excluded middle I have not gone into the modifications which Brentano according to Oskar Kraus made after the turn of the century, partly because it is difficult to know how far Kraus' interpretation, which is based on letters and notes, which Brentano has not himself published (he lost his eyesight in 1903), is correct.
69. This is not to deny the importance of Marxism as a challenge. See e.g. H. Stuart Hughes: *Consciousness and Society. The Reconstruction of European Social Thought 1890-1930* (1958) Vintage Books, Random House, N. York 1961, in particular Ch. 3.
70. Although Talcott Parsons' interpretation of Durkheim, Weber and Pareto in *The Structure of Social Action* (1937) has been critizised with justice, this main point is, I think, still valid.
71. Reprinted *Gesammelte Politische Schriften*. München 1921, pp. 7-30.
72. Weber's report was published in 1892 in Vol. LV of *Schriften des Vereins für Sozialpolitik*. A good account of the investigations is given in Reinhard Bendix: *Max Weber. An Intellectual Portrait*. Anchor Books, N. York 1962, pp. 14-23 and 41-48.
73. "Die optische Täuschung, als gäbe es selbständige ökonomische ... Ideale, wird freilich als solche klar, sobald man an der Hand der Literatur unserer Wissenschaft diese 'eigenen' Grundlagen der Bewertung zu ermitteln sucht. Ein Chaos von Wertmassstäben teils eudämonistischer, teils ethischer Art, oft beider in unklarer Identifikation, tritt uns entgegen." Weber: *Gesammelte Politische Schriften*, pp. 21-22.
74. First edition by Marianne Weber 1922. I use the third edition, editied by Johannes Winckelmann, Tübingen 1968.
75. Verlag Schober, Stuttg. 1865.
76. This is not quite correct. In some cases Liebmann writes "Es muss etc.", and it is only at the end of the chapters in which he critizises the four main lines of development in post-Kantian German philosophy between which he distinguishes (the idealist one (Fichte, Schelling, Hegel), the realist one (Herbart), the empiricist one (Fries) and the transcendent one (Schopenhauer)) that he concludes in this way.
77. This is true of Cohen and Natorp, but not of a younger member of the school, Ernst Cassirer (1874-1947). His main works in the philosophy of the humanities came, however, after 1920.
78. See Weber: *Gesammelte Aufsätze zur Wissenschaftslehre* (1922) 3. Aufl. 1968 (GAW), pp. 291-383 (papers from 1907).
79. See Wilhelm Windelband: *Präludien. Aufsätze und Reden zur Einführung in die Philosophie* (1884) 2. Aufl. Tübingen 1903, pp. 119-54.
80. See Windelband: *Präludien*, pp. 1-57.

81. It is the first part of *Kritik der praktischen Vernunft* Erster Teil, Erstes Buch, Zweites Hauptstück.
82. Heinrich Rickert: *Die Grenzen der naturwissenschaftlichen Begriffsbildung* (1902) 3. Aufl. Tübingen 1921.
83. Quoted from Thomas Burger: *Max Weber's Theory of Concept Formation*. Duke Univ. Press 1976, p 10. On the relationship between Rickert and Weber see also Guy Oakes: *Weber and Rickert. Concept Formation in the Cultural Sciences*. The MIT Press, Cambr., Mass. 1988.
84. See GAW pp. 146-214: "Die 'Objektivität' sozialwissenschaftlicher und sozialpolitischer Erkenntnis" (Engl. transl. in M.W.: *The Methodology of the Social Sciences*. The Free Press of Glencoe 1979, pp. 49-112.).
85. It is clear that the way Rickert – and Weber – distinguishes between natural and human or cultural sciences builds upon Windelband's distinction between nomothetic and ideographic sciences, but, as Rickert emphasizes, the distinction is purely methodological, not based on substantive differences between the realm of nature and that of the mental or the cultural. Consequently we can have a natural (nomothetic) science of the human mind; psychology is in Rickert's opinion to a great extent nomothetic. And we can have idiographic sciences of natural phenomena; what is called "natural history" is often of this kind. Regarding economics Weber to some extent changed position. In the inaugural lecture he declared himself "a younger member" of the German historical school whose leader Gustav Schmoller dominated "Verein für Sozialpolitik". In the methodological papers he, however, critizised this school and tried to find a middle way between its conception of economics as a purely historical (ideaphic) science and Carl Menger's conception of it as nomothetical. The notion of ideal type concepts by which he transcends Rickert's theory of concept formation, is his main tool for delineating this middle way position.
86. This, of course, is a problem for Weber too. I tend to agree with the criticism of the theory of value relevance put forward by W.G. Runciman in his *A Critique of Max Weber's Philosophy of Social Science*. Cambr. Univ. Press 1972, particularly on pp. 37 sqq.
87. Heinrich Rickert: *Die Probleme der Geschichtsphilosophie* (1904) 3. Aufl. Heidelberg 1924, p. 60, quoted from Oakes: *Weber and Rickert*, p. 86.
88. See Oakes, *op. cit.* p. 31. The best expression of Weber's perspective is the "Vorbemerkung" he wrote to his *Gesammelte Aufsätze zur Religionssoziologie* (Vol 1, 1920, pp. 1-16).
89. See Rickert: *Die Grenzen...*, pp. 245 sqq.
90. See Rickert: *Die Grenzen...*, pp. 513 sqq.
91. "Vom System der Werte", pp. 295-327 in *LOGOS* IV (following right after Weber's paper "Über einige Kategorien der verstehenden Soziologie").
92. Heinrich Rickert: *System der Philosophie. Erster Teil: Allgemeine Grundlegung der Philosophie*. Tübingen 1921. (RS)
93. RS 102-08.
94. RS 109.
95. RS 112.
96. RS 126.
97. RS 123-24.
98. RS 116.
99. RS 143.
100. RS 134.
101. RS 132.

102. This is the main thesis of Sven Edvard Rodhe: *Über die Möglichkeit einer Werteinteilung.* Lund 1937.
103. RS 132-37.
104. See RS 353-54.
105. See Rickert: Vom System der Werte, *LOGOS* IV *passim* or RS pp. 350 sqq.
106. See e.g Oakes: *op. cit.* pp. 39-40 & 145-46.
107. Roger Brubaker: *The Limits of Rationality. An Essay on the Social and Moral Thought of Max Weber.* George Allen & Unwin, Lond. 1985.
108. "Die Unmöglichkeit "wissenschaftlicher" Vertretung von praktischen Stellungsnahmen ... ist prinzipiell deshalb sinnlos, weil die verschiedenen Wertordnungen der Welt in unlöslichem Kampf untereinander stehen" GAW 603.
109. "Es handelt sich nämlich zwischen den Werten letzlich um unüberbrückbar tödlichen Kampf, so wie zwischen 'Gott' und 'Teufel'." GAW 507.
110. "Jede empirische Betrachtung dieser Sachverhalte würde, wie der alte Mill bemerkt hat, zur Anerkennung des absoluten Polytheismus als der einzigen ihnen entsprechenden Metaphysik führen." GAW 507.
111. See e.g. GAW 506.
112. *Politik als Beruf* is reprinted in *Gesammelte politische Schriften*, München 1921, pp. 396-450. English translation in H.H.Gerth and C Wright Mills, eds.: *From Max Weber. Essays in Sociology* (1946) Galaxy, N. York 1958, pp. 77-128. It may be more correct to describe the conflict as one between the two kinds of ethics which Weber calls "Gesinnungsethik" and "Verantwortungsethik".
113. See H.H.Bruun: *Science, Values, and Politics in Max Weber's Methodology.* Munksgaard, Copenhagen 1972.
114. See Stephen P. Turner & Regis A. Factor: *Max Weber and the Dispute over Reason and Value.* Routledge & Kegan Paul, Lond. 1984, pp. 32-35.
115. Brubaker: *The Limits...*, ch. 3.
116. "Stammler tritt als Vertreter das "kritischen Idealismus" auf: sowohl auf ethischen wie auf erkenntnistheoretischen Gebiet wünscht er sich als echtesten Jünger Kants anerkannt zu werden" GAW 293.
117. He had a rather inferior position and only got a chair in 1914, in Strassburg. On his life and career see e.g. David Frisby: *Georg Simmel.* Ellis Horwood Ltd., Chichester & Tavistock Publ., Lond. 1984, the introduction by Donald N. Levine to the Simmel-volume in the series The Heritage of Sociology (*Georg Simmel on Individuality and Social Forms*, Univ. of Chic. Press 1971) or the chapter on Simmel in Lewis A Coser: *Masters of Social Thought* (1971) 2. ed. Harcourt Brace Janowich, N. York 1977.
118. See Frisby *op. cit.* p. 35.
119. "Der Unterschied zwischen der Erscheinung und dem Ding an sich, wie er bei Kant auftritt, wird meist sehr missverständig für metaphysisch gehalten ...Es handelt sich nicht um den Gegensatz von Vorstellung und Nicht-Vorstellung, sondern um den zwischen empirischem und rein intellektuellem Vorstellen. Kant hat die Kritik der reinen Vernunft ... geschrieben ... um zu zeigen, dass alle unsere Erkenntniss an Sinneseindrücke als Material gebunden ist" Simmel: *Einleitung in die Moralwissenschaft.* 2. Bd. Wilhelm Hertz, Berlin 1893, p. 149.
120. I shall not go into the difficult questions of who influenced whom or to what extent each has devopled his ideas independently, inspired by Kant and other earlier thinkers.
121. See Georg Simmel: *The Problems of the Philosophy of History.* Transl. and ed. by Guy Oakes. The Free Press, N. York 1977, p. 80.

122. Simmel *op. cit.* p. 83.
123. See Simmel *op. cit.* p. 98.
124. See Simmel *op. cit.* pp.76-77.
125. See Horst Jürgen Helle: *Soziologie und Erkenntnistheorie bei Georg Simmel*. Wissenschaftliche Buchgesellschaft, Darmstadt 1988 p. 107. Helle quotes from the autobiographical fragment published in Kurt Gassen & Michael Landmann, hrsg.: *Buch des Dankes an Georg Simmel*, Berlin 1958.
126. This conception is already suggested in *Über sociale Differenzierung* (1890), but most clearly set forward in *Grundfragen der Soziologie* (1917).
127. "Dass wir etwas sollen, lässt sich, wenn es logisch erwiesen werden soll, immer nur durch Zurückführung auf ein andres als sicher vorausgesetztes Sollen erweisen; ..." Simmel: *Einleitung.* 1. Bd. 1892, p. 12.
128. Georg Simmel: *Philosophie des Geldes* (1900) 7. Aufl. Duncker & Humblot, Berlin 1977 (G). English translation by Tom Bottomore & David Frisby: *Philosophy of Money*. Routledge & Kegan Paul, Lond. 1978 (M).
129. G 3, M 59.
130. G 5, M 60-61.
131. Gustav Schmoller, according to Frisby p. 93, in a review of *Philosophie des Geldes* (*Jahrbuch für Gesetzgebung, Verwaltung und Volkswirtschaft,* 25, 1901) relates that "on the 20th of May 1889 (Simmel) delivered a paper on the 'Psychology of Money' in my political science seminar". Simmel returned to the phenomena of money in several publications in the following years, until the book in 1900 was finished. In 1899 'philosophy' had been substituted for 'psychology' in the title, and the work had become one which "strives to be a philosophy of the whole of historical and social life" (Letters to Bouglé quoted by Frisby p. 93).
132. "Damit würde ich mich schon zufrieden geben ... wenn nicht ... tatsächlich absolute u. objektive Werthe Anspruch auf Anerkennung machten. Die Lösung dieser Schwierigkeit, die ich für manche Fälle gefunden habe, versagt bei anderen, und ich sehe auch kein Ende der Schwierigkeiten ab, denn ich halte allerding daran fest, dass ich bei meinem Relativismus nur bleiben kann, wenn er alle die Probleme, die sich die absolutistischen Theorien stellen, gleichfals zu lösen imstande ist." Letter of May 10 1898, published in Gassen & Landmann, hrsg.: *Buch des Dankes*, p. 94.
In a letter of July 19 the same year Simmel tells Rickert that he now "sees land" (*op. cit.* p. 95).
133. G 7-8, M 63.
134. G 8-11, M 63-65.
135. G 11-13, M 65-67.
136. G 13, M 67.
137. G 14, M 67.
138. The German words used are "Forderung" and "Anspruch". See G 14-15, M 68-69.
139. G 15, M 68.
140. G 16, M 69.
141. In his last work *Lebensanschauung* (Duncker & Humblot, München & Leipzig 1918) he in chapter 2 describes these spheres as autonomous.
142. G 412-18, M 376-80.
143. In America, on the contrary, the University of Chicago already from its start in 1892 had a department of sociology, and others followed. Albion Small who organized the Chicago

department translated several papers by Simmel and published them in the *American Journal of Sociology* which he started in 1895.
144. The title of his paper was: *Soziologie der Vergesellschaftung* (Sociology of Sociation). See Frisby *op. cit.* p. 15.
145. According to a study by T.S.Simey (*Sociological Review* 14, 1966) referred to in Turner & Factor, *op. cit.* p. 57,it was the "passion for bureaucracy of the conservatives" in the "Verein" he attacked. One may here refer to his discussion on productivity (*Über die Produktivität der Volkswirtschaft*, repr. pp. 416-23 in his *Gesammelte Aufsätze zur Soziologie und Sozialpolitik*. Tübingen 1924, in which he declared that the reason why he with such an extraordinary sharpness turned against any confusion "des Seinsollens" with "dem Seienden" was not that he underrated questions "des Sollens"; on the contrary, it was because he could not stand that problems of the greatest ideal consequences were treated as technical question within a special discipline. And he said that particularly the members of the "Verein" were guilty of this error (*op. cit.* p. 419).
146. Published in *LOGOS* VII, 1917, repr. in GAW 489-540. English translation (The Meaning of "Ethical Neutrality" in Sociology and Economics) pp. 1-47 in Max Weber: *The Methodology of the Social Sciences*. Transl. and ed. by Edward A Shils and Henry A. Fich. The Free Press of Glencoe 1949.
147. See Frisby *op. cit.* p. 17.
148. Ferdinand Tönnies: *On Social Ideas and Ideologies*. Ed. transl. and annotated by E.G. Jacoby. Harper & Row, N. York 1974, pp. 199-200.
149. See Jeffrey T. Bergner: *The Origin of Formalism in Social Science*. Univ. of Chic. Press 1981, pp. 91-95.
150. Ferdinand Tönnies: *Community & Society (Gemeinschaft und Gesellschaft.*Transl. and ed. by Charles P. Loomis,(1957) Harper & Row, N. York 1963, p. 141.
151. V. Pareto: *The Mind and Society* (1935) Dover Publ., N. York 1963, § 2110. (PM)
152. Raymond Aron: *Main Currents in Sociological Thought*, Weidenfeld and Nicolson, Lond. 1968, vol. 2, p. 146.
153. PM §§ 2129-30. This situation has been named after Pareto: *Pareto optimality*.
154. PM §§ 2121-2124. See also Raymond Aron, *op. cit.* vol. 2, p. 147.
155. PM §§ 2131-2135.
156. PM § 2137.
157. One might e.g. have included G.E.Moore, who introduced the term "intrinsic value" for the property of being "good in itself", and who in the preface to *Principia ethica* (Cambr. Univ. Press 1903, p. X-XI) pointed out similarities between his own theory and that of Brentano. Also the Polish philosopher-sociologist Florian Znaniecki is of great interest in this conncetion. In the famous "Methodological note" which he wrote for *The Polish Peasant in Europe and America* (co-authored with William I. Thomas. First published 1918-20) he introduced and defined a concept of value which he considered central to sociological theory.
158. Allen Barton: *Measuring the Value of the Individual*, pp. 5, 62-96 in *Religious Education*, Research Supplement July-August 1962, in particular p. 5, 63. Barton introduces four other important distinctions, among which some coincide with those I have mentioned. Among the others are "values as desires" versus "values as obligations" and "values as attributes of individuals" versus "values as attributes of collectives".
159. See Nicholas Rescher: *Introduction to Value Theory*. Prentice-Hall. N.J. 1969.
160. Everett W. Hall: *What is Value? An Essay in Philosophical Analysis*. Routledge & Kegan Paul, Lond. 1952.

161. See Mogens Blegvad: Indledningsforedrag om begrebsdannelsesproblematik, pp. 28-55 in *Rapport om forskningsfeltet "Værdiopfattelser og værdisystemers udvikling"*. Udvalget vedrørende værdiopfattelser og værdisystemers udvikling, København, juni 1978.

THE CORRESPONDENCE OF ERNST MACH WITH A YOUNG DANISH PHILOSOPHER

CARL HENRIK KOCH

University of Copenhagen

I

In the autumn of 1907 the young Danish philosopher Anton Thomsen (1877-1915), a pupil of Harald Høffding (1843-1931), visited Vienna together with his wife Ada Adler (1878-1946), a classical scholar, with the intention of attending philosophical and sociological lectures and establishing useful connections with philosophers and classicists in Vienna. Anton Thomsen was especially eager to meet Friedrich Jodl (1849-1914), one of the best-known representatives of German positivism at the turn of the century. It seems that, originally, Thomsen had no plans for visiting Ernst Mach (1838-1916), but one of Mach's friends, the indologist Leopold von Schroeder (1851-1920), who, incidentally, was also a friend of Thomsen's uncle, the famous Danish philologist Vilhelm Thomsen (1842-1927), urged him to see Mach. Thomsen did so, but wasn't impressed. In his diary he wrote under date of Dec. 3, 1907:

> Payed Ernst Mach a visit. He is very kind, but deaf. Talked to him for half an hour *(My translation)*.[1]

No more, no less.

Thomsen doesn't seem to have realized that Mach was a world-famous philosopher and historian of science. He met him after what Blackmore has called "the thirty year's war"[2] between Mach and Ludvig Boltzmann (1844-1906) concerning atomism, had ended with the untimely death of Boltzmann, and a year before the outbreak of the "war" against Max Planck (1858-1947). Certainly, in 1907 Mach wasn't a philosophical or a scientific relict.

A few days after Thomsen's visit, Mach sent him a very polite letter (Dec. 6, 1907), in which he apologized for his infirmities and for not being able to return the visit. Back in Copenhagen, Thomsen answered Dec. 29, 1907. The correspondence continued up to Thomsen's premature death September 18th., 1915, just 18 days after he had succeeded to Høffding's chair of philosophy at the University of Copenhagen. 16 letters and post-cards; one in Mach's own hand,[3] the other typewritten and signed with Mach's facsimile stamp, are preserved at the Royal Library in Copenhagen,[4] and 13 letters and post-cards from Thomsen to Mach are to be found in the records of the Ernst-Mach-Institut in Freiburg.

It is surprising that Mach initiated a correspondence with Thomsen. The young Dane was mainly interested in the history of philosophy – in 1905 he had defended his thesis on Hegel's philosophy up to 1806, and later he wrote a lengthy book on Hume (1911), which was translated into German in 1912.[5] But he also planned to write a descriptive psychology based on the "law of parsimony". In his letters to Mach he showed only a superficial knowledge of Mach's philosophy of science, and he seemed to have read Mach only after his stay in Vienna. Later, about 1913, Thomsen was mainly interested in Mach's support in gaining Høffding's chair. Høffding, who had been Thomsen's friend, turned against his former pupil in 1911. In a review of Thomsen's book on Hume, Høffding criticized the author for his attack on religion and religious feelings, and described Thomsen as a very immature person without any deeper understanding of the human soul.[6] In a booklet on religion and the science of religion, Thomsen in return criticized Høffding's philosophy of religion.[7] Høffding assumed the essence of religious belief to be a belief in the constancy of values. But this is nonsense, Thomsen says, because believers do not perceive the content of their belief in that way. Høffding was furious and in 1913, 70 years old, he decided to stay on as a professor in order to prevent Thomsen from getting his chair. In this situation Thomsen appealed to Mach, and Mach wrote a letter of recommendation in which he also made some remarks about his own intellectual career.

From a philosophical or scientific point of view, the correspondence between Mach and Thomsen – perhaps a coming man in Danish philosophy – is not very interesting. The old well-established scientist certainly had sympathy for his young friend, partly perhaps because both of them were attacked by theologians and religious enthusiasts. But some of Mach's letters contain matters of interest, especially in connection with his relation to William James (1842-1910),[8] and they all testify to his generosity.

Five of the eight letters from Mach, which are published in this article, and the excerpts from Thomsen's diary and from his letters to Mach, have never appeared in print before. I have retained the spelling and the punctuation of the letters.

II

Very early in the century, Thomsen had discussed religious matters with Høffding. Thomsen saw in Høffding's philosophy of religion nothing but a masked form of Christianity, and in his diaries he criticized Høffding in very vehement terms. James' pragmatic vindication of religious belief was rejected too. In his diary Thomsen wrote Jan. 14, 1908:

... Read James' pragmatism. It makes me sick with vexation *(My translation)*.

Thomsen viewed both Høffding's philosophy of religion and James' pragmatism as modern forms of irrationalism and as a reaction to a modern scientific world picture.

In 1908, Mach had probably sent Thomsen the new edition of his lecture on the relative educational value of the classics and the sciences in high schools.[9] Thomsen thanked him in a letter now lost, dated Jul. 18, 1908. Mach replied:

Hochgeehrter Herr College!
Durch Ihr Schreiben vom 18/VII haben Sie mich sehr erfreut. Ich danke Ihnen auch sehr, dass Sie meine Forderungen in Bezug auf die Beschränkung des altsprachlichen Unterrichts gemässigt finden. Diese würden noch gemässigter erscheinen, wenn mein Vortrag nicht vor 20 Jahren, zurzeit der Alleinherrschaft der klassischen Philologie, sondern heute gehalten worden wäre.

Ich würde es für ein grosses Unglück halten, wenn das Bewusstsein des Zusammenhanges unsere heutigen Kultur und unserer heutigen Weltanschauung mit der antiken erlöschen würde. Dazu, damit dies nicht geschieht genügt es, wenn ein Teil der Menschen, diejenigen, welche dafür begabt sind, die antiken Sprachen und Literaturen gründlich studirt, und die Ergebnisse dieses Studiums den andern überliefert. Selbst Lateinisch und Griechisch kann fast jeder soviel lernen, dass er die Autoren im Original lesen kann. Dazu ist aber nicht eine achtjährige Quälerei nötig, die fast jedes andere Studium unterdrückt.

Davon, dass die philologischen und naturwissenschaftlichen Disciplinen einander feindlich gegenüber stünden, kann natürlich nicht die Rede sein; dieselben unterstützen sich vielmehr gegenseitig, wenn auch leider häufig die Vertreter der einen mit unglaublicher Borniertheit den Vertretern der andern gegenüberstehen. Man sollte aber endlich anerkennen, dass die Befähigungen für beide Gebiete zugleich sehr selten sich in einem Kopfe zusammenfinden, und dass es eine zwecklose, unnötige Graumsamkeit ist, Leute, deren Beruf und Studienrichtung in jungen Jahren schon entschieden ist, ihre schönste Jugendzeit mit berufsfremden Studien zu belasten und zu vergeuden. Deshalb preise ich die Schulverfassung in Dänemark. Ich glaube, dass sich dieselbe, wenn auch erst nach manchen Abänderungen und Versuchen, bewähren wird. Namentlich in Oesterreich, welches doch wesentlich ein Agrarstaat ist, haben wir ein Bedürfniss nach solchen Einrichtungen. Was sollen wir mit den vielen Leuten anfangen, welche nur Lateinisch und Griechisch lesen können, denen aber die übrige Welt fremd ist.

Als interessantes Beispiel möchte ich Ihnen mitteilen, dass in unserem Wiener philosophischen Professorencollegium vier ausgezeichnete Naturforscher und Mathematiker sitzen, welche im Gymnasium an den philologischen Gegenständen Schiffbruch gelitten haben, dh durchgefallen sind. Ich selbst habe mein Latein auf dem Lande unter Leitung meines Vaters spielend durch vieles Autorenlesen erlernt, und lese noch sehr viel, teils zur Belehrung, teils zur Unterhaltung. Die drei obersten Klassen des Gymnasiums machte ich öffentlich, und empfand manche Stunde geradezu als Kerkerhaft, da mein Beruf schon entschieden war. Vom Griechischen dieser letzten Gymnasialzeit habe ich heute fast nichts mehr übig. Wenn Sie mich auch 20 Jahre lang unterrichten würden, würde aus mir doch kein Philologe. Die Anlagen sind eben, und zum Glück, verschieden. Mit Gomperz, Jerusalem und v. Schroeder[10] treffe ich jetzt nicht mehr zusammen; die sind wol schon über alle Berge; nur mich hält eben meine Lähmung fest.

Mit nochmaligen herzlichen Dank für Ihren freundlichen Brief und hochachtungsvollen Grüssen an Sie, Ihre Frau Gemalin und Prof Höffding

Ihr stets ergebener

Wien 24/VII' 08   Dr. Ernst Mach

In 1909 Mach had sent the new edition of *Die Geschichte und die Wurzel des Satzes von der Enthaltung der Arbeit* to Thomsen. In a letter of thanks, dated Aug. 30, 1909, Thomsen wrote among other things:

> Seit einigen Jahren habe ich gedacht über die descriptive Psychologie von Gesichtpunkt d. Gesetz d. Sparsamkeit zu schreiben, d.h. eine genaue Distinction zwischen die psychologischen 1) Grundgesetze (z.B. d. Associationsgesetz), 2) Grundbegriffe (z.B. Focus d. Bewusstseins = Aufmerksamkeit, Wiedererkennen u.s.w.) 3) und abgeleite Begriffe durch zu führen. Nach dieser Ordnung wird das Willensbegriff ganz verschwinden, und die ganze Psychologie d. Gefühls geändert werden.

A paper on Hume's *Natural History of Religion* published by Thomsen in *The Monist*, was enclosed.[11]

Mach answered:

> Hochgeehrter Herr College!
> Herzlichen Dank für Ihre Hume-Abhandlung und Ihre freundlichen Zeilen vom 30/8. Meine Publication von 1872[12] ist natürlich recht unvollkommen, abgesehen davon, dass diese Fragen damals mit einer grossen Reserve den Naturforschern gegenüber behandelt werden mussten. Ich hielt auch damals den Oekonomiegedanken noch für originell. Nicht nur latent, sondern auch deutlich ist er zu finden z B bei Newton, Adam Smith u A.[13] Vier Jahre später erschien Avenarius' Schrift "Über das Denken der Welt nach dem Prinzip des kleinsten Kraftmasses".[14] Ausführlicher ist das Kapitel "Oekonomie der Wissenschaft" in meiner Mechanik.[15] Es ist zwar erst 1883 erschienen, aber schon 1873

entworfen und teilweise geschrieben. Ich glaube in der Tat, den Oekonomiegedanken für ein gesundes Prinzip aller Wissenschaft halten zu dürfen, gerade deshalb, weil er so oft und unabhängig von verschiedenen Menschen gefunden worden ist.

Was Sie über Psychologie sagen, gefällt mir sehr. Am besten scheint mir von den gegenwärtigen Büchern: W James, the Principles of Psychology, New York, 1890, sowol was die Tatsachendarstellung als was die Theorie betrifft. Wie schwach ist dagegen manches neuere Buch! Dass James etwas zu Schwärmerei und Spiritismus neigt, kann man ihm seinen andern Leistungen gegenüber zu gut halten.

Th Gomperz hat eben den dritten und letzten Band seines prächtigen Buches "Griechische Denker" vollendet.[16] Im verflossenen Jahre haben wir viele Schulreform-Debatten und Vorträge gehabt. v. Arnim und Ostwald haben sich da als gleich aber entgeengesetzt beschränkt, beziehungsweise einseitig erwiesen.[17] Ich habe oft an die Unterredung mit Ihnen gedacht.

Indem ich bitte mich auch Ihrer gelehrten Frau Gemalin zu empfehlen, in besonderer Hochachtung Ihr ergebenster

Wien 4/9' 09   Dr. Ernst Mach

In a letter dated Jul. 25, 1910 Thomsen renewed his criticism of James:

Ich muss sagen, dass ich einen bestimmten Unterschied mache zwischen die oekonomische Erkenntnistheorie und den amerikanischen Pragmatismus. Die erste, von Avenarius, Maxwell – aber philsophisch doch gewiss am Besten von Ihnen vertreten, wendet wirklich wissenschaftlich das Gesetz der Sparsamkeit an: der Werth einer Hypothese ist ihr wissenschaftlicher Arbeitswerth. Die andere dagegen erweitert dieses: die wissenschaftliche Werth wird was überhaupt fördert. Wo Ihr Richtung nur die Wissenschaftlichen Werth betrifft, geht der Pragmatismus zu der persönlichen Werth über – wie Sören Kierkegaard bei uns gesagt hat: Die Wahrheit ist was mich erbaut.[18] Nach dem Gesetz der Sparsamkeit trifft bei allen metaphysischen Problemen eine "Deproblematisierung" ein, James dagegen macht eine neue Metaphysik nach "consensus omnium" oder besser nach "consensus Americanorum" mit "mind-cure", "christian science" u.s.w. Er geht von der wissenschaftlichen Wahrheit zu dem, was Kierkegaard "die persönliche Wahrheit" genannt hat.[19] Er ist mir, nachdem ich seiner "Pragmatismus"[20] gelesen habe, innerlich wiederwärtig. Der alte Theismus in modernen Aufzug, "american Humbug" ohne alle geschichtliche Kenntnisse. Ich schreibe jetzt eine grössen Monographie über Hume, deren ersten Band in Februar 1911 erscheinen soll (200 Jahre nach Humes Geburt). Dieser Band betrifft nur sein Leben, seine Psychologie und Erkenntnistheorie, das zweite Band wird seine Ethik und Religionsphilosophie behandeln. Ich hoffe dass ich es einmal deutsch oder english übersetzen lassen kann, und es wird mir dann eine grosse Freude sein, Ihre Kritik zu hören. ... Höffding geht es gut, er hat eben eine grössen Darstellung der Erkenntnistheorie vollendet, die – ich glaube in October – erscheinen wird.[21] Haben Sie Cassirers grosse geschichtliche Dartellung gelesen;[22] sie hat mir in vielen Beziehungen grosse Freude gemacht. ...

Mach replied:

> Hochgeehrter Herr College!
> Besten Dank für Ihren freundlichen Brief vom 25/7' 10.
> Meine persönlichen Erinnerungen an W James sind sehr angenehme; er hat mich noch in Prag 80 oder 81 besucht.[23] Ich erinnere mich keines Mannes, mit dem ich trotz der Divergenz der Ansichten, doch so gut und fruchtbringend hätte discutiren können. Er opponirte mir fast überall und doch gewann ich fast überall durch seine Einwendungen. Schon damals hütete er sich vor jedem Tropfen Wein oder Caffee, so dass ich ihn mehr für einen ängstlichen Hypochonder als für einen wirklich kranken Mann hielt. Der Schwerpunkt seiner Arbeit liegt gewiss in seiner ausgezeichneten Psychologie. Mit seinem Pragmatismus kann ich mich nicht ganz befreunden. "Wir dürfen den Gottesbegriff nicht fallen lassen, weil er uns zu viel verspricht".[24] Das ist ein etwas gefährliches Argument. "Nicht nur der Gesunde muss immer die beste Einsicht haben".[25] Das hat auch sein Richtiges, doch wäre es traurig, wenn das Urteil der Gesunden durch die Kranken dirigirt würde. Die Welt muss doch vor allem den Gesunden verständlich sein. Was Sie über Ihre und Høffdings Arbeiten schreiben, interessirt mich sehr. Leider fällt mir das Lesen in dänischer Sprache sehr schwer.
> Ich bin überhaupt sehr schwerfällig und eingesogen geworden, war in den letzten zwei Jahren überhaupt nicht mehr in der Akademie,[26] habe auch Prof v Schroeder nicht mehr gesehen. – Aus meiner letzten kleinen Abhandlung,[27] die Ihnen wol zugegangen ist, sehen Sie, dass ich mich gegen Angriffe wehre, so lange ich überhaupt noch mitreden kann, was ja bald aufhören muss. Mit hochachtungsvollen Grüssen an Ihre Frau Gemalin und Sie, hochgeehrter Herr College, Ihr ergebenster
>
> Wien 21/I' 11   Dr. Ernst Mach

Mar. 19, 1911 Thomsen sent his new book on Hume (in Danish) to Mach, and wrote *inter alia* in relation to Mach's last letter:

> Ihr Brief hat mich ausserordentlich interessirt; die Auffassung von James, die Sie hier skizzirt haben ist ungefähr auch die meinige. So viel ich weiss hat er um 1892 eine Krisis durchgemacht,[28] und nachher ist eine bestimte Seite viel stärker hervorgetreten – nämlich die mystisch-religiöse, die Interesse an mind-cure u.s.w. Seine späteren Arbeiten, nachdem er Schule gemacht hat, sind mir zuwider. Nachdem diese Richtung c 1900 auch bei Höffding stärker hervorgetreten ist, ist auch James bei uns kanonisiert worden, und es hat Höffding sehr geärgert, dass wider diesen Kultus von verschiedenen Seiten Einsprüche erhoben worden sind. Wenn Höffding über James schreibt – namentlich wenn es gegen mich geschieht – muss ich stets hören, dass Sie für den amerikanischen Pragmatismus Burgschaft geleistet haben. Dies ärgert mich, weil ich auf sehr vielen Cardinalpunkten mit Ihnen ganz einverstanden bin und der ökonomischen Erkenntnistheorie die grösste Bedeutung zumisse.

Mach thanked Thomsen Mar. 23, 1911.[29] In his letter, he noted the election of the first woman as member of the Norwegian parliament:[30]

> Es geht doch im Norden mächtig vorwärts, während man sich hier Encyclica, Antimodernistenneid und andere Dummheiten gefallen lässt.

In his next letter, Thomsen had the following comment on Mach's remark:

> Sie loben die nordischen Verhältnisse, aber in der Wirklichkeit sind die politische Verhältnisse in Dänemark sehr traurig; der Parlamentarismus hier seit 1901 hat nur, und nur, Schade gestiftet. Eine übermächtige Katholische Kirche haben wir glücklicherweise nicht; aber unsere Bauerpartei hat das land d. Abgrund nahe gebracht. Die Männer unserer Demokratie haben schlecht genug gethan – Gott behüte uns für die Weiber.[31]

Sometime during the summer Thomsen must have told Mach about his attempt to have his book on Hume translated into German. Mach wrote back Jun. 5, 1911[32] saying that it was difficult for him to read Danish and that he should be happy to read the book in German. He also told Thomsen news from the philosophical congress in Bologna. Sep. 22, 1911 Thomsen wrote again to Mach. In his letter he mentioned the political situation in Vienna. Mach replied:

> Hochgeehrter Herr College!
> Die Unruhen in Wien sind in den auswärtigen Zeitungen jedenfalls übertrieben dargestellt worden. Es war nichts, als eine ruhige ernste Kundgebung der sozial-demokratischen Partei beabsichtigt. Die Leute, die sich haufenweise erschiessen lassen müssen, sobald ein Diplomat, der nur die Interessen einer winzigen Minorität im Auge hat, einen dummen Streich begeht, wollen doch nicht auch zur Unterhaltung der Regierung *verhungern*. Mit mehr Umsicht vorher und etwas Takt nachher, hätte man sich den ganzen Spektakel ersparen können. Mit welchen Gefühlen die Herrn Leute zu Kerkerstrafen verurteilen werden, die durch den unzeitgemässen und unklugen Gebrauch der Waffen zu den Excessen gereizt worden sind, kann man sich denken.
> Meine Schrift nochmal zu lesen, möchte ich Ihnen bei Ihren dringenden Geschäft nicht zumuten; ich hatte nur das Bedürfnis Ihnen für Ihr schönes Geschenk auch wieder etwas zu senden. Uebrigens bin ich jetzt auch sehr beschäftigt als Flickschuster meiner Verleger durch neue Auflagen alter Schriften.
> Das schöne und anregende Buch von Höffding habe ich das erstemal durchgelesen, kann aber jetzt nicht dabei verweilen, da hierzu die Ruhe fehlt.
> Meine Tochter,[33] die diesen Sommer mit ihrer Familie auf Usedom war, hat von dortaus einen Ausflug nach Kopenhagen gemacht. Sie sollte dann noch nach Christiania und Bergen mit ihrem Mann, musste aber, da sie die Seereise schlecht vertrug, einige Tage in Kopenhagen bleiben. Sie hat von der Stadt, den Bewohnern, den Museen die angenehmsten Eindrücke. Für mich ist es mit dem Reisen längst vorbei.

Für Ihr freundliches Schreiben, das mir immer Vergnügen macht, bin ich Ihnen sehr zu dank verpflichtet, umsomehr als mein ganzer Verkehr bei meiner Taubheit sich fast auf den brieflichen beschränkt.
Mit hochachtungsvollen Grüssen an Ihre Frau Gemalin, Ihr Sie hoch schätzender College

Wien 29/IX' 11   Dr. Ernst Mach.

Mar. 27, 1913 Thomsen wrote to Mach asking for a recommendation. In his letter he also complained about an attack in public from religious quarters and told Mach about his intention to seek employment in the USA or Germany:

27/3 1913
Hochgeehrter Herr Hofrat!
Verzeihen Sie, bitte, gütigst, dass ich mich an Sie mit dem Ersuchen wende, mir in einer für mich sehr wichtigen Angelegenheit zu helfen. Verschiedene schwierige Universitätsverhältnisse hierzuland haben bewirkt, dass im Jahre 1913 nicht diejenige Vakanz eingetreten ist, die bestimmt hätte erwarten werden mussen. Es sind – unter uns gesagt – mein eigener Onkel, Excellenz Wilh. Thomsen, und Professor Höffding, die nicht der allgemeinen Gepflogenheit haben folgen und sich beim erfüllten 70. Lebensjahr zurückziehen wollen.[34] Viele Jahre hat man mich hingehalten, und ich habe, um existieren zu können, jedes Frühjahrssemester 8 bis 11 Stunden täglich reden müssen. Oft sogar mehr. Jetzt sind aber meine Aussichten ins ungewisse hinausgeschoben worden, und ich habe mir noch dazu in den letzten Jahren durch das viele Dozieren eine Hals-Krankheit zugezogen, die bewirkt, dass ich es nicht mehr lange auf diese Weise aushalten kann. Hierzu kommt überdies noch, dass man jetzt wegen meines Buchs über Hume und wegen eines kleineren Buchs, "Religion und Religionswissenschaft", wovon ich in ein paar Monaten Inhen die deutsche Ausgabe überreichen zu können hoffe sowohl von philosophischer als namentlich von klerikaler Seite alles tut um mir wissenschaftlich und wirtschaftlich zu schaden. Meine Stellung hierzuland ist so schwierig, dass ich Schritte getan habe um in Amerika oder am liebsten in Deutschland mich um einen Lehrstuhl zu bewerben. Ich richte nun die Bitte an Sie, die Sie ja einige Kenntniss von meiner Produktion haben, dass Sie mir eine Empfehlung geben wollen, die so abgefasst wäre, dass sie sowohl in Amerika, Deutschland als in Dänemark benützt werden könnte.
Leider ist die Situation eine solche, dass ich, wenn ich nicht von Ausland Hülfe bekommen (deshalb brachte ich u.a. so viele Opfer, damit "Hume" in Deutschland herausgegeben werden könnte), in meiner Heimat ganz still von den Dünkelmännern wissenschaftlich und wirtschaftlich wird vernichtet werden.
In der Hoffnung auf Ihre Hülfe und mit besten Dank für Ihre letzte freundliche Karte, bin ich Ihr mit verzüglicher Hochachtung ergebenster

Anton Thomsen.

Mach replied:

> Hochgeehrter Herr College!
> Ihr Schreiben vom 27/III habe ich heute erhalten. Ich war durchaus nicht weit verzogen, sondern nur einige Häuser weiter, auch polizeilich wol angemeldet. Der Postvermerk auf Ihrem Brief-umschlag war also eine faule Ausrede. Noch muss ich hinzufügen, dass ich im vorigen Sommer in Folge eines Sturzes zu meiner rechtseitigen apoplektischen Lähmung einer linksseitige traumatische Lähmung acquirirte, die mich fast 5 Monate bettlägerig erhielt. Ich fange eben an gehen zu lernen, was für meine beabsichtigte Umsiedlung nach München sehr fatal ist.
> Ich staune über Ihre Nachrichten. Also auch bei Ihnen eine klerikale Partei! Tout comme chez nous. Man lässt auch unsere Privatdozenten recht lange warten. Aber wenigstens nützt man sie nicht so unverantwortlich aus, wie bei Ihnen. Auch wird bei uns ein Professor mit 70 Jahren nicht gefragt, ob er etwa noch weiter dienen will, sondern einfach pensionirt und das ist das einzig Richtige.
> Was nun Ihre Angelegenheit betrifft, so wird es zweckmässig sein, ich um Apperturen umzusehen. Darüber bin ich, längst nicht mehr activ, wenig orientirt. In Marburg ist Cohen in Ruhestand getreten,[35] dort wird man aber wol exklusiv kantisch sein. In München ist seit langer Zeit Lipps schwer krank[36] man kann sich aber nicht entschliessen ihn gegen seinen Willen zu pensioniren. Der recht frische Hans Cornelius[37] aus der berühmten Künstlerfamilie wurde so wie Sie jahrelang hingehalten und mit blossen Versprechungen vertröstet, bis er endlich vor 2 Jahren an die höhere Handelshochschule in Frankfurt a M abging, wo er sich ganz wol befindet.
> Wie man sich in Deutschland durch die verschiedenen lokalen philos Kliken durchwinden soll, weiss ich vorläufig noch nicht. Ich würde an Ihrer Stelle meinen Blick Amerika, dem lande der unbegrenzten Möglichkeiten zuwenden. Vielleicht würde es mir dort eher gelingen, einen Anknüpfungspunkt zu gewinnen. Es gibt dort noch nicht viele Philosophen; man hört dort einen *weiter* als in Deutschland. Die Philosophen sind dort vorwiegend experimentelle Psychologen, Ethnographen etc. Mich würde das locken.[38] Lassen Sie mir einige Tage Zeit zu überlegen. Es ist mir vor 2 Jahren gelungen einen in Deutschland studierenden jungen Norweger an der Universität Christiania gegen einen Konkurrenten anzubringen. Freilich wurde ich, von dort aus gefragt.[39] Das gelingt nicht immer so leicht. Diesem Brief folgt bald ein zweiter von Ihrem hochachtungsvoll ergebenem
>
> Wien 11/IV,13   Dr. Ernst Mach

And a few days later:

> Hochgeehrter Herr College!
> Indem ich mich anschicke das von Ihnen gewünschte Schriftstück zu verfassen, bitt ich Sie mir, ohne sich im geringsten einen Zwang aufzulegen, die Daten aufzuführen, die Ihnen selbst als massgebend erscheinen, um einer Anspruch auf eine Professur an einer deutschen oder nordamerikanischen Universität zu begründen. Ich habe die deutsche Ausgabe des Humebuches mit Interesse und Vergnügen durchgenommen. Ich habe den

Eindrück einer sehr tüchtigen historischen und kritischen Arbeit gewonnen. Meine Aufgabe würde sehr erleichtert, wenn ich mich, durch die Erfüllung des oben ausgesprochenen Wunsches in der Stand gesetzt sehen würde, auch andere Ihrer Arbeiten zu berücksichtigen.

Sollten Ihre Leute Sie wirklich fortziehen lassen, nachdem Sie so Ihre Kräfte missbraucht haben? Sollte Ihre Unterrichtsverwaltung dies zugeben?

In bezug auf Deutschland bitte ich nicht zu viel von meiner Person zu erwarten. Man hält mich da für einen Physiker, der sich in die Philosophie verirrt hat und wurde kaum gestatten, dass ich irgendwo habilitire. Man sagt das nicht offiziell, aber man erfährt es durch kleine Indiskretionen.

In Amerika ist mein Name etwas besser angeschrieben. Man hat mich im verflossener Jahr zum Ehrenmietglied der New York Academy of Sciences gewählt mit ausdrücklichen Hinweis auf meine Erkenntnislehre.

Nun, wie es auch sei; so will ich hoffen, dass ein Wink von auswärts genügt, Ihre Situation zu stärken.

Mit hochachtungsvollem Gruss Ihr ergebenster

Wien, 15/IV,13.   Dr. Ernst Mach.

A week later Mach had read parts of the German translation of Thomsen's book on Hume:

Hochgeehrter Herr College!
Zunächst möchte ich Ihnen gestehen, dass der persönliche Eindruck, den ich vom Humes Treatise erhalten habe, doch deutlich von demjenigen abweicht, der Ihrer Kritik entspricht. Wenn ich Book I, Sect VI, Of personal identity aufschlage und dort lese: For my part, when I enter most intimately into what I call myself, I always stumble on some particular perception or other ... I never can catch myself ... usw bis zum Schluss des Absatzes. Wer so denkt, ist mit einemmal das ganze quälende Phantom der persönlichen Unsterblichkeit los; er ist sofort religiös frei; er versteht die grösste Kulturerscheinung des Orients, den Buddhismus. – Hätte Kant jemals so gedacht, seine Psychologie und auch seine Erkenntnistheorie wäre eine andere geworden. Dass Hume diese Stellen geschrieben hat, wenn er auch nicht im ersten Anlauf eine haltbare Erkenntnistheorie geschaffen hat, müsste ich ihm sehr hoch anrechnen.

Als meine Analyse der Empfindungen durch die englische Uebersetzung von 1897 in Kalkutta bekannt wurde,[40] welche ähnliche Stellen über das Ich schon auf den ersten Seiten enthält, erkannten die Buddhisten deren Brauchbarkeit als buddhistische Propagandaschrift und übersetzten sie in ihre Sprachen.[41] Dies tröstete mich vollkommen über den Misserfolg des Buches in Deutschland.

Kants Prolegomena ergriffen mich allerdings mächtig in meiner Jugend durch die entschiedene Abweisung aller Metaphysik. Man wird aber sehr abgekühlt, durch den Missbegriff des "Dinges an sich" und durch das Wiedereinschleichen der Metaphysik. Kant hat allerdings die Newtonschen Arbeiten studirt. Wie hat er sie aber verstanden? In den metaphysischen Anfangsgründe der Naturwissenschaft, beschäftigt er sich mit den falschen, sinnlosen Begriffen der absoluten Zeit und das absoluten Raumes, ohne dieselben los zu werden, während Newton wenigstens durch seinen naturwissenschaftlichen Takt davor bewahrt wird, von solchen Phantome eine ernste Anwendung zu machen. Und welche Missverständnisse bringt Kant vor ? Die Trägheit ist ihn einfach Leblosigkeit. Dasselbe kehrt noch bei dem Kantianer Appel[42] im 19. Jahrhundert wieder. Nie habe ich begriffen, warum Begriffe, wie Ursache und Wirkung, die Hume so gut als empirisch aufgedrängte erkannt hat, nun durchaus überempirische sein sollen ? Hume hat mit der ersten Zeile aufgehört Scholastiker zu sein; Kant ist es immer geblieben.

Ihr Buch über Hume wird in Deutschland sehr viel Sympathien finden denn nur die wenigsten deutschen Philosophen haben wie Fries[43] und Beneke[44] schüchterne Versuche gemacht, sich von Kant zu befreien, ohne dass Ihnen dies ganz gelungen wäre. Auch die Anmerkung über James in Ihren deutschen Buch S 380-384 wird in Deutschland volle Sympathie finden.[45] In Amerika wäre es ein Fehler auf letztere hinzuweisen, da man James als eine sehr liebenswürdige Persönlichkeit hoch achtet. Eine gewisse Unsicherheit in religiösen und spiritistischen Fragen ist in Amerika, aber auch in England, allzu verbreitet.

Jedenfalls eignen sich zu Ihrer Empfehlung in Deutschland und Amerika nur zwei im Ton verschiedene Schriften. Meine subjektiven Ansichten haben natürlich *nichts damit zu tun*. Schwieriger ist aber die Frage, in welcher Form man diese Schriften an den Mann bringt und diese ist wieder in Deutschland, wo man alle Philosophie gepachtet zu haben glaubt, schwieriger zu beantworten als in Amerika.

Bitte, sagen Sie, hochgeehrter Herr College, wie Sie sich den Vorgang ungefähr denken. Mit hochachtungsvollem Gruss von Ihrem ergebenstem

Wien, 22/IV,13.   Dr. Ernst Mach

In May Mach wrote to Thomsen about his problems with the religious party i Vienna in 1895. Incidentally, he describes his difficulties in almost exactly the same terms as he had used in a similar letter to Joseph Popper-Lynkeus (1838-1921) about twenty years earlier:[46]

Hochgeehrter Herr Doctor!
Als ich für Wien primo et unico loco für Geschichte u Theorie der inductiven Wissenschaft, für mein selbst beschränktes Programm, vorgeschlagen war, erhielt ich von vertraulicher Seite aus dem Ministerium Nachricht, dass eine "liberale College" dort meine Schriften vorgelegt, zuvor aber die antiklerikalen Stellen angestrichen habe. – Ich fand noch stärkere antiklerikale Stellen, strich auch diese an und sendete die Schriften an das Ministerium mit einem Brief des Inhalts: Ich bin zwar kein antiklerikaler Agitator, kann aber nicht in Büchern, in welchen ich das Resumé meiner Lebensarbeit niederlege, den Standpunkt der "epistolae obcurorum virorum" einnehmen. Sollte man dies jedoch wünschen, so bitte ich von meiner Ernennung abzusehen. Nach einigen Tagen kam meine Ernennung während 30-40 Jahre vorher Widerruf gefordert wurde. Es bessern sich also doch die Verhältnisse, selbst im klerikalen Oesterreich. In Dänemark muss es doch besser sein.

Erst gestern erhielt ich meine Schreibmaschine. Ich habe wenig Zeit, viel zu schreiben, bin auch durch meine apoplektische und hinzugekommene traumatische Lähmung gehindert. Wenn Sie mich unterstützen wollen, so bitte ich eine ausführlicheres

Schriftstück abzufassen, das ich gern unterschreibe, nachdem ich das Buch gelesen habe. Mit hochachtungsvollem Gruss Ihr ergebenster

München 22/V 1913   Dr. Ernst Mach

Mach's recommendation was enclosed:

Dr Anton Thomsen über David Hume.
Schreiber dieser Zeilen erfuhr von der Existenz Humes zuerst durch das bekannte Zitat Kants.[47] Damals machte dies Zitat, wie überhaupt Kants kritischer Idealismus einen tiefgehenden Eindruck auf ihn. Dann aber nahm Kants Einfluss allmälig ab, als dem Schreiber klar wurde, dass es mit der gänzlichen Elimination der Metaphysik nicht so ernst gemeint sei. Zuerst wurde das "Ding an sich" als eine überflüssige und zwecklose Erfindung erkannt, wodurch Berkeleys Betrachtung, die bei Kant immer latent mitspielt an Wertschätzung gewann. Der Blick wandte sich jetzt wieder Locke, Berkeley und Hume und der letztere als jener erkannt wurde, welcher die Absicht hatte mit der Metaphysk am gründlichsten aufzuräumen.

Von Hume lernte ich erst "Enquiry" in der mangelhaften deutschen Uebersetzung Kirchmanns um 1880[48] und dann "Treatise" im Original um 1897 kennen, wobei mir immer noch der Eindruck blieb, dass lezteres Werk den grössten philosophisch-antimetaphysischen Aufschwung enthält. Dieser Eindruck blieb nicht nur mir, sondern den in Humes Richtung weiter arbeitenden Philosophen der modernen Zeit: R Avenarius, dessen Erläuterer J Peztoldt[49] und dem von Kant ausgehende W Schuppe,[50] wo in ihren Wegen äusserst nahe zusammengehen.

Ich muss nun sagen, dass von meinem starken Vorurteil für Hume Dr Anton Thomsen, mich gründlich befreit und geheilt hat, wofür ich ihm sehr dankbar bin. Es war aber nur einem Mann wie Thomsen, der die ganze antike Literatur, sowie die Werke der modernen Vorgänger und Zeitgenossen Humes gründlich kannte und beherrschte möglich nachzuweisen, wie viel Hume den Philosophen Locke, Berkeley auch Hobbes verdankt. Wenn Hume es bei einem Anlauf bewenden lassen musste und wenn er sich mit einer unvollkommenen Psychologie begnügen musste, statt sich zu einer fruchtbaren Erkenntnistheorie zu erheben, so liegt dies an Humes Unbekanntschaft mit den Naturwissenschaften und insbesondere mit Mathematik. In Kenntnis dieser Gebiete konnte er mit Descartes, Leibniz und Kant nicht concurriren; seine Auffassungen gewannen keine haltbare Form.

In dem ersten Band von Thomsens "David Hume, sein Leben und seine Philosophie" machen wir die Bekanntschaft eines ungemein belesenen, gelehrten Mannes von hoher kritischer philosophischer Schulung, der seine Ansichten in überzeugender Weise vorzubringen und zu begründen weiss. Wir können ihm nur wünschen, dass ihm sein Heimatsland, Deutschland oder Nordamerika bald eine Professur der Philosophie anbietet, die dieser ausgezeichneten Lehrkraft Gelegenheit zur vollen Wirksamkeit gibt.

In dem vorliegenden ersten Band seines Werkes äussert Thomsen die Ansicht, dass der Name David Hume mit stets zunehmendem Glanz in der Geschichte der Wissenschaften strahlen wird; sein Buch solle aber nicht den Förderer der Erkenntnistheorie feiern, sondern den grossen Aufklärer, der das innerste Wesen der Religion erklärte.

Wien 22/V 1913.   Dr. Ernst Mach.

In a letter dated May 27, 1913 Thomsen expressed his gratitude and asked why Mach had moved from Vienna to Munich. Mach replied Jun. 1, 1913, the last letter that has been preserved.[51] The last known letter from Thomsen to Mach is dated Mar. 29, 1915. Half a year later Thomsen was dead.

III

In his biography on Mach, J.T. Blackmore – apparently not aware of the letters from Mach to Thomsen – says that Niels Bohr (1885-1962) may have been influenced by Mach through Anton Thomsen.[52]

Through his wife Thomsen was close to the Bohr family. He discussed philosophical matters with Christian Bohr (1855-1911), a friend of Høffding and the father of Niels Bohr. Once he reports in his diary that he had discussed "various philosophical problems with Niels and Harald" (Jan. 3, 1911) – Harald was Niels Bohr's younger brother, the matematician Harald Bohr (1887-1951), from 1915 a professor at the Technical University of Denmark.

It is not very likely that Thomsen was able to give Niels Bohr an adequate impression of Mach's philosophy of science. Thomsen's books and articles contain only a few references to the philosophical or methodological thoughts of Mach.[53] Thomsen's knowledge of modern science was also very scanty. He was Niels Bohr's senior by eight years, and his diaries do not reveal any recognition of the genius of the future Nobel Prize winner. In his epistemology Thomsen was a pupil of Høffding, like his master an old-fashioned positivist in the tradition of Comte and Mill, and in metaphysics a realist. He shared Mach's interest in descriptive psychology which he considered the true scientific psychology. But the epistemological discussions in his book on Hume are determined by Høffding's rather peculiar views on the foundation and growth of human knowledge. As a philosopher, Thomsen had learned nothing from Mach.

Notes
1. Thomsen's diaries are preserved in the files of Thomsen's papers and letters at the Royal Library in Copenhagen, shelf mark N.kgl.S. 4703, 4°.
2. J.T. Blackmore: *Ernst Mach, His Work, Life and Influence*, Berkeley 1972, pp. 204 f.
3. A post-card, not dated but most likely from May 1913.
4. The letters from Mach to Thomsen (Royal Library, Copenhagen, shelf mark N.kgl.S. 4703, 4°) are dated 06.12.1907, 24.08. 1908, 04.09.1909, 21.01.1911, 23.03.1911, 05.06.1911,

29.09.1911, 1912 ? (Post-card), 11.04.1913, 15.04.1913, 22.04.1913, 30.04.1913, (Post-card), May 1913 ? (Post-card), 22.05.1913, 01.06.1913, 1913 ? (Post-card). The letters dated 04.09.1909, 21.01.1911, 23.03.1911, 05.06.1911, 22.04.1913, 01.06.1913 have been published by J. Blackmore and Klaus Hentschel in *Ernst Mach als Aussenseiter*, Wien 1985.
5. A. Thomsen: *David Hume, Sein Leben und seine Philosophie*, (Erster Band), Berlin 1912.
6. *Nordisk Tidsskrift* 1911, pp. 77-84.
7. A. Thomsen: *Religion og Religionsvidenskab*, Copenhagen 1911, in German: *Religion und Religionswissenschaft*, Berlin 1913.
8. On Mach's relation to James, cf. R.B. Perry: *The Thoughts and Character of William James*, I-II, London n.d. (the preface is dated 02.05.1935), *passim*.
9. *Über den relativen Bildungswert der philologischen und der mathematisch-naturwissenschaftlichen Unterrichtsfächer*, Wien 1908, originally published 1886.
10. Th. Gomperz 1832-1912, classicist and historian of philosophy; W. Jerusalem 1854-1923, philosopher; L. von Schroeder 1851-1920, indologist.
11. A.Thomsen:"David Hume's Natural History of Religion" – in *The Monist* XIX, 1909, pp. 269-88.
12. E. Mach: *Die Geschichte und die Wurzel des Satzes von der Erhaltung der Arbeit*, Prag 1872.
13. Cf. E. Mach: *Die Mechanik historisch-kritisch dargestellt*, 9. Aufl., Leipzig 1933, p. 469.
14. R. Avenarius (1843-96): *Philosophie als Denken der Welt gemäss dem Princip des kleinsten Kraftmasses*, Hab. Schr., Leipzig 1876.
15. Cf. Mach, *op.cit.*, pp. 457-471.
16. Th. Gomperz: *Griechische Denker* I-III, Leipzig 1893-1909.
17. Hans von Arnim 1859-1931, classical scholar. Wilhelm Ostwald 1852-1932, chemist and philosopher of science. Ostwald wrote against the pedagogical principles of the New Humanism in *Grosse Männer*, Leipzig 1909, pp. 342 f. Von Arnim's contribution to the discussion has not been localized.
18. Søren Kierkegaard 1813-1855 Thomsen is referring to Kierkegaard's well-known conception of truth as subjectivity, cf. his *Concluding Unscientific Postscript*, transl. by D.F. Swenson, Princeton 1941, p. 182.
19. "An objective uncertainty held fast in an appropriationprocess of the most passionate inwardness is the truth, the highest truth attainable for an existing individual", *loc.cit.*
20. W. James: *Pragmatism*, New York/London 1907.
21. H. Høffding: *Den menneskelige Tanke*, Copenhagen 1910 (*Der menschliche Gedanke*, Leipzig 1911).
22. E. Cassirer 1874-1945, *Das Erkenntnisproblem* I-II, Berlin 1906-07.
23. James travelled in Europe from August 1882 to March 1883, cf. Perry, *op.cit.*, I, pp. 586 f.
24. Cf. James' remarks in *Pragmatism*, London 1913, pp. 106 f. and p. 299.
25. Cf. James *op.cit.* pp 292 f. and his *The Meaning of Truth*, London 1909, pp. 228-29, where he remarks in relation to pluralism that: "It lacks the wide indifference that absolutism shows. It is bound to disappoint many sick souls whom absolutism can console. It seems therefore poor tactics for absolutists to make little of this advantage. The needs of sick souls are surely the most urgent, and believers in the absolute should rather hold it to be great merit in their philosophy that it can meet them so well". Mach's implicit characterization of James' pragmatism is not fair. James in general argued against absolutism and for pluralism.
26. Mach was a member of Die kaiserlische Akademie der Wissenschaften in Vienna.
27. Presumably "Die Leitgedanken meiner naturwissenschaftlichen Erkenntnislehre und ihre Aufnahme durch die Zeitgenossen" – in *Physikalische Zeitschrift* 11, 1910, pp. 599-606 (also

in *Scientia* 7, 1910, pp. 225-40), Mach's reply to the criticism of Planck in "Die Einheit des physikalischen Erkenntnis" – in *Physikalische Zeitschrift*, 10, 1909, pp. 62-75.
28. James experienced a personal crisis in 1870-72, cf. Perry *op.cit.* I, pp. 322 f. and II, p. 324 where he writes that "there is also a close relation between James' view of religious conversion (in *The Varities of Religious Experiences*,1902) and his own "crisis" in 1870-72".
29. Published in Blackmore and Hentschel, *op.cit.*, p. 90.
30. Anna Georgine Rogstadt 1854-1938, member of the Norwegian parliament 1911-12.
31. Women were enfranchised in Denmark in 1915.
32. Published in Blackmore and Hentschel, *op.cit.*, p. 92.
33. Caroline Mach 1873-1965, married to Anton Lederer 1870-1932.
34. Høffding and Vilhelm Thomsen were close friends. The Feuerbach scholar Wilhelm Bolin 1835-1924, who corresponded with Anton Thomsen, wrote in a note that Vilhelm Thomsen didn't like his nephew, cf. K. Sorainen: "Wilhelm Bolin och Danmark" – in *Finsk Tidsskrift* 123, 1937, p. 118.
35. H. Cohen 1842-1918, from 1876 professor of philosophy in Marburg, founder of the Neo-Kantian school of Marburg.
36. Th. Lipps 1851-1914, from 1894 professor of philosophy in München.
37. H. Cornelius 1853-1947, from 1910 professor in Frankfurt a. M.
38. Mach's interest in anthropology and ethnology is attested in his last book *Kultur und Mechanik*, Stuttgart 1915, cf. Blackmore *op.cit.*, pp. 270 f.
39. Anathon Aall 1867-1943. Recommended by Mach, Høffding and the Norwegian professor of philosophy Arne Löchen 1850-1930, Aall was appointed professor of philosophy at the University of Christiania (Oslo) 29.02.1908, cf. *Det kongelige Frederiks Universitets Aarsberetning for 1907-1908*, Kristiania 1909, p. 4.
40. *Contribution to the Analysis of Sensations*, Chicago 1897.
41. A translation to Pali (?) is not registered in Thiele's bibliography in E. Mach: *Die Geschichte und die Wurzel* etc., Nachdruck Amsterdam 1969. On Mach's relation to Buddhism, cf. Blackmore, *op.cit.*, pp. 286-99.
42. Perhaps Max Apel 1869-1945. His *Kants Erkenntnistheorie* was published in 1895.
43. Jakob Friedrich Fries 1773-1843.
44. Friedrich Eduard Beneke 1798-1854.
45. In a footnote, Thomsen writes that "...Das Neue im "Pragmatismus" sind nur die Namen, die leeren Worte. Seit der Zeit des Hegelianismus gibt es keinen, der mit so steifer, nichtsagenden und zumeist ganz kindischen Rubriken operiert wie James (p.381) ... Es soll frei heraus gesagt werden: der "Pragmatismus" ist ein alter Bekannter, der europäische Obskurantismus, nur im modernen amerikanischen Gewande und mit allen Phrasen von Wahltribünen und Erweckungspredigten ausgerüstet. Sein Ziel ist die Wissenschaft im Namen der Wissenschaft zu unterminieren" (p. 383).
46. Cf. Blackmore, *op.cit.*, p. 153.
47. At the age of 15, Mach read Kant's *Prolegomena*, which made a powerfuld impression upon him, cf. *Die Analyse der Empfindungen*, 6. Aufl., Jena 1911, s. 23. The only quotation from Hume in Prolegomena is found in the preface, where Kant misquotes from the essay "Of the Rise and Progress of the Arts and Sciences" on the relative value of metaphysics and natural science in a monarchy, cf. D. Hume: *Essays, moral, political and literal*, London 1903, p. 127. Probably Mach has in mind Kant's famous dictum that it was Hume who interrupted his dogmatic slumber.
48. German translation by J.H. Kirchmann, Berlin 1869. Mach probably read this translation in a later edition.

49. Joseph Petzoldt 1862-1929. In his *Einführung in die Philosophie der reinen Erfahrung* I-II, Leipzig 1899-1904, Petzoldt gave a popular presentation of the empirio-criticism of Avenarius.
50. W. Schuppe 1839-1913. Mach's *Erkenntnis und Irrtum* (1905) was dedicated to Schuppe.
51. Published by Blackmore and Hentschel *op.cit.*,pp. 117-18.
52. Blackmore *op.cit.*, p. 314.
53. Thomsen refers to Mach in *David Hume*, Berlin 1912, pp. 383-84, where he writes that "Es wäre wünschenwert, wenn der bedeutende Vorkämpfer der ökonomischen Erkenntnistheorie, Ernst Mach, einmal entschieden Stellung zu dem amerikänischen "Pragmatismus" nehmen und uns damit vor dieser Verfälschung der wissenschaftlichen Werte retten wollte".